**ELECTING
JIMMY
CARTER**

ELECTING JIMMY CARTER *The Campaign of 1976*

Patrick Anderson

LOUISIANA STATE UNIVERSITY PRESS

Baton Rouge and London

Copyright © 1994 by Louisiana State University Press
All rights reserved
Manufactured in the United States of America
First printing
03 02 01 00 99 98 97 96 95 94   5 4 3 2 1

Designer: Laura Roubique Gleason
Typeface: Janson Text
Typesetter: G & S Typesetters, Inc.
Printer and binder: Thomson-Shore, Inc.

Library of Congress Cataloging-in-Publication Data
Anderson, Patrick, 1936–
    Electing Jimmy Carter : the campaign of 1976 / Patrick Anderson.
        p.   cm.
    Includes index.
    ISBN 0-8071-1916-4 (acid-free paper)
    1. Presidents—United States—Election—1976. 2. Carter, Jimmy,
1924–   . 3. United States—Politics and government—1974–
1977. I. Title.
E868.A53   1994
324.973′0925—dc20   94-28320
                                                                    CIP

For Barbara Woodward

CONTENTS

**ELECTING
JIMMY
CARTER**

INTRODUCTION:
A HIGH-WIRE ACT

During the 1976 presidential campaign, from mid-May through the November election, I was Jimmy Carter's chief speechwriter. When we parted after the election, he asked me to write an authorized book on his administration. Instead, I wrote the first draft of this memoir, drawing on vivid memories and extensive notes. Throughout the campaign, I almost always carried a notebook, to jot down my exchanges with the candidate and ideas for his speeches. Beyond that, it was my instinct as a novelist and journalist to record all I could of the drama around me.

After completing the draft, I put it aside, in part because my wife was working in the White House, and when I looked for it a few years later, I couldn't find it. The manuscript was lost and stayed lost for more than a decade.

In 1992, my son was digging in the attic and found my copy under several layers of debris. At the time, I was living at the Playboy Mansion in Los Angeles, working with Hugh Hefner on his autobiography. One day I barred my door against marauding Playmates and read my long-lost account of our long-ago campaign. I confess I found it fascinating—who *was* that reckless lad?—and sent a copy to my friend Hugh Graham, a professor of history at Vanderbilt University, who encouraged me to publish it. Now, after many years, and some updating, my buried treasure finally sees the light.

Be warned: What follows is no scholarly treatise. It is, rather, an intensely personal, partisan, novelistic view of Jimmy Carter and his first race for president. Those six months were the most exciting, emotional, challenging time of my life. I've tried to convey the blood and guts of our political odyssey—the chaos, conflict, and despair, as well as the friendships, shared passions, and moments of achievement that made it bearable, at times glorious. I've tried to be honest, about myself and others. I've tried, however imperfectly, to make the telling worthy of the experience.

The campaign was a magnificent adventure—variously a crusade, a party, and an ordeal. Our candidate may have been a saint, but he surrounded himself with sinners. Robert Scheer wrote in *Playboy* that Jody Powell, Hamilton Jordan, Jerry Rafshoon, Greg Schneiders, Pat Caddell, and I were "as hard-drinking, fornicating, pot-smoking, freethinking a group as has been seen in higher politics." We accepted his praise with our accustomed modesty. We were a ragtag band of outsiders determined to take back America—and to enjoy ourselves in the process.

I met Carter by chance, admired him at first, but came to have decidedly mixed feelings about him, as everyone close to him did. He was our hope and our despair, leader and loose cannon, Machiavelli and Mr. Rogers. Hiding behind his big smile and pieties about love and peanut farming was a far more interesting and complex man than the voters ever knew. He possessed not only intelligence and high moral purpose but a mixture of pride and piety that could make him quite maddening to deal with. I found much to respect in the candidate and much to regret in the man.

Carter was above all else a different candidate. He defined himself thusly, as southerner, Baptist, peanut farmer, naval officer, nuclear physicist, friend of Bob Dylan and fan of Dylan Thomas, politician who would never lie, the entire long and sometimes dubious litany. His differences made him intriguing, but as the campaign wore on the question became how different he could be and still be elected.

Carter was running far less on what he had done, as a one-term governor, than on what he said, as a colorful, quotable newcomer to national politics. The man was verbal to a fault, often fascinating but sometimes hitting sour notes. He alarmed various groups with a reference to "ethnic purity," by speaking of "Eyetalian" voters, and by invoking "brotherhood" before a roomful of feminists. But it was the infamous *Playboy* interview that threw our campaign into chaos, as Carter's remarks on lust and sin revealed for the first time how alien his thinking was to millions of voters.

By then, his campaign had become a high-wire act. Our man was up there in the spotlight with no net below him, dancing about, turning his daring flips, leaping to the left, bobbing to the right, dazzling the crowd but forever threatening to tumble into the void.

Ultimately, Carter couldn't sustain his high-wire act. He squeaked by in 1976, but America tired of his flip-flops and his preaching and by 1980 we were eager to embrace a smooth-talking snake-oil salesman who did not disturb us with talk of sin and sacrifice.

Clearly, Carter was a better president than the rhetoric of the Reagan years suggested, and he has become a much-admired ex-president, yet I think he is no better understood today than when he first emerged on the national scene two decades ago. He remains an enigma, high-minded and self-serving, liked or disliked for superficial reasons, never quite coming into focus.

In Carter's hometown of Plains they have a saying about him: After an hour you love him, after a week you hate him, and after ten years you start to understand him. More than ten years have passed since our victorious campaign and the flawed presidency that followed, and it is time to look more closely at this proud, driven, and contradictory man. This is how he looked to me.

1
FIRST IMPRESSIONS

I met Jimmy Carter quite by accident.

In the 1970s I lived with my wife, Ann, and daughter, Laura, in the village of Waterford, Virginia, an hour's drive west of Washington. One Sunday in February of 1975, our neighbors Gus and Faye Hewlett invited us over to meet some people who were coming out from Washington for the afternoon. Among them were an attractive couple in their thirties, Peter Bourne and Mary King, who proved to be the Washington representatives of Jimmy Carter, the former governor of Georgia who had recently announced his candidacy for president.

I knew little of Carter, but Peter and Mary were veterans of the anti-war and civil-rights movements, and I was impressed as they praised his record on race, prison reform, education, and drug treatment. Ann was from Atlanta, I from Fort Worth, and we were delighted to see a progressive southerner running for president. All that spring and summer, we followed the occasional news reports on the Carter campaign with special interest. We'd never met the man, but already we were pulling for him.

In August, after I finished writing a political thriller called *The President's Mistress*, an editor of the *New York Times Magazine* called and asked if I'd like to profile either Vice President Nelson Rockefeller or Senator Pat Moynihan.

"Those guys have been written to death," I said. "How about Jimmy Carter? I hear he's interesting."

Soon I was headed South. I spent two days in Atlanta, talking to Carter's friends and advisers, two more days traveling with the candidate in Florida, and a final day at his home in Plains. What follows are snapshots from that hectic week, first impressions of the longshot candidate who the next year, against all odds, would become president.

The candidate's confidence

I first glimpsed Carter at 2 P.M. on Tuesday, August 26, at Jerry's Restaurant in the Bradenton/Sarasota airport. I had flown down with Jody Powell, Carter's press secretary. Jody was in his late twenties, a good-looking, sandy-haired, chain-smoking, powerfully built man who still looked like the high school athlete he once had been. Carter spent twenty minutes fielding reporters' questions, then spoke to perhaps two dozen local supporters. I was impressed by his obvious intelligence, by the contrast between his mild manner and his sharp tongue, by his unconventional rhetoric, and most of all by his absolute self-confidence.

Jimmy Carter was going to be the next president. He told you so, with no ifs, ands, or buts. He would enter all the primaries, he would not settle for vice president, and he intended to win. The man's audacity was stunning. You could have gotten 100-to-1 odds against him, yet somehow you didn't laugh. He left you with an unsettling feeling that he knew something you didn't.

Which, in a way, he did.

The candidate's humor

The national media would in time declare that Carter had no humor. That was not my observation. Almost the first thing I heard him say was his deadpan response to a young woman who asked who his running mate would be: "I won't give you a name, but I'll tell you the qualities she'll have."

Carter had two standard laugh lines on that trip. One was to solemnly declare that he believed he could be a good president despite the handicap of not being a lawyer.

The other was his Amy joke: "After Mrs. Ford made her remarks about her daughter's affair, reporters asked how Mrs. Carter and I would feel if we found out our daughter was having an affair. Well, we would be deeply hurt and shocked . . . because our daughter Amy is only seven years old!"

Remember the Amy joke; we will return to it.

The candidate's rival

It was imperative that Carter defeat George Wallace in the Florida primary and thus demonstrate that he, not the Alabama segregationist, spoke for the South. Carter often mentioned his rival. Playing off the Wallace campaign slogan, Carter would say: "Let's not send them a message—let's send them a president."

"Wallace is a perennial candidate," Carter would add. "I suspect he'll still be running in 1988, if he's able."

Then, lest anyone suspect that "if he's able" implied that the crippled Wallace had a health problem, he would quickly add, "And I assume he will be."

Carter often commented that Wallace ran very strange campaigns— "He raises a lot of money and spends very little"—then he would drop the subject, leaving each listener to ponder for himself the mysteries of George Wallace's finances.

The blonde at the bar

We arrived that first evening at a place called the Cove Inn Club in the resort town of Naples. This wasn't your corner tavern where the Archie Bunker crowd gathered to guzzle beer and cuss the government. The Cove Inn Club was sleek and dark and expensive, and was packed with well-heeled Floridians who'd come to examine this peanut farmer who aspired to lead the Free World.

The evening went routinely—the Amy joke, an attack on the mess in Washington, a swift reminder that he wasn't responsible for that mess—until the blonde at the bar spoke up. She was tanned, ponytailed, fortyish, and mad as hell.

"What're you gonna do about all those welfare cases who've already bankrupted New York City and Dee-troit and Washington, D.C.?" she demanded.

"I'm glad you asked that," replied Carter, the very soul of reason. "I think the first thing we have to do is separate those who can work from those who can't."

"They don't *want* to work," the lady protested. "I've talked to people on welfare who *enjoy* it!"

"The statistics show that only about 10 percent of the people on welfare are able to work," the candidate insisted. "The rest are children or mothers or . . ."

"I don't believe that," the blonde snapped.

"Well, perhaps you'd better believe your statistics and I'll believe mine," Carter suggested, and began to outline his welfare position, which included "compassion and respect" for those who couldn't work.

"But they don't *want* to work," the woman persisted, as people began to shush her and mutter that she was drunk.

"I disagree with you about the quality of people on welfare," Carter replied, and talked about the welfare mothers his programs had put to work in Georgia. But the blonde raged on about bankrupt cities until Carter cut her off with the comment that either he didn't understand her question or her question wasn't understandable.

It had gotten a bit tense in the Cove Inn Club. I suspected that plenty of those cabin-cruiser Democrats shared the blonde's views on welfare and her implicit racism. I scribbled in my notebook, "Good—stubborn—stuck to his guns."

A few minutes later, on the drive to our motel, I had my first chance to interview Carter. He proved to be in a lousy mood. Maybe he was tired. Maybe the exchange with the woman had angered him. Maybe he knew that the motel we were headed for was inhabited mostly by bugs. When I

opened with the easiest possible question—to describe his political support around the country—he snapped that he couldn't violate confidences
by answering that. I said I only wanted the names of those like Andrew
Young and Dr. Martin Luther King, Sr. (names he'd been dropping all
day) who were openly supporting him. Again he said he couldn't violate
confidences. At the time I was mystified. Later, I decided he was irritated
because he had precious little political support then, and what he had was
more liberal than he liked to admit.

Trying to get the interview on track, I asked his position on amnesty
for those who'd resisted service in Vietnam.

"I want to get all that behind us," he said. "But I don't want to say
the draft evaders were right and put them on the same footing as the men
who fought."

I asked if he would give resisters a dishonorable discharge.

"No, nothing that severe. No punishment."

"I don't see what you have in mind," I admitted.

"I haven't worked it out yet," he said impatiently. "I'm not a lawyer. I
can't articulate it for you right now."

I had to smile. All day he'd been scoring cheap laughs off lawyers, and
now he was ducking my question by saying he wasn't one. This was a man
who liked to have it both ways.

The candidate's poetics

The next morning I interviewed Carter as a small plane carried us from
one Florida town to another. Not wanting to rile him again, I tossed a
real softball: what books did he like? He mentioned James Agee's *Let Us
Now Praise Famous Men* and the novels of William Faulkner. His aides had
said he was a fan of both Bob Dylan and Dylan Thomas, and in answer to
my question, he said *Blonde on Blonde* was his favorite Bob Dylan album—
my favorite, too. Then he told how he'd discovered Dylan Thomas:

"Fifteen or twenty years ago, on a slow day at my peanut warehouse, I
was reading an anthology of poetry and came across Thomas' 'A Refusal
to Mourn the Death, by Fire, of a Child in London,' with its final line,

'After the first death, there is no other.' That struck me. I didn't understand it. My son Jack and I got a book of Thomas' poetry from the library and as a family exercise we would read his poems and try to figure them out. Later I got the records of Thomas reading them.

"In July of 1964, during a special session of the Georgia legislature, several other state senators and I would sometimes sit around in the afternoons and listen to those records. There was one senator who'd known Thomas personally. He was a very rich fellow whose father owned the largest paper mill in Georgia. After college he'd lived in Greenwich Village and known Thomas there.

"When I ran for governor for the first time, I made a mistake. The Atlanta *Constitution* was opposing me. In a speech about the environment, I quoted Thomas' 'The Force That Through the Green Fuse Drives the Flower.' A reporter from the *Constitution* wrote a snide article about it, one that made me look silly. I learned to be more careful about what poems I quoted."

I was fascinated, for I'd never associated the Georgia legislature with the poetry of Dylan Thomas. But after we landed I overheard Carter telling Jody that he didn't want any more airborne interviews, because it was too hard on his voice.

A Kiwanis luncheon

Carter spoke that day to a luncheon meeting of the Downtown Kiwanis Club in Tampa. I was not in the best of moods as I sat there listening to them singing "I'd Rather Be in Kiwanis" to the tune of "For He's a Jolly Good Fellow." Yet Carter was beautifully attuned to the Florida bankers and druggists and insurance agents who surrounded him. He presented himself, not as a visitor from far-off Washington, but as a candidate whose double-knit suit and Georgia drawl were not unlike their own, as a small businessman who spoke their language in more ways than one.

Carter was introduced as "a great American" and greeted with a standing ovation. He responded with what his staff called his "Two Questions" speech, which summed up his still-evolving campaign themes. He said the

American people had been "deeply wounded" by Vietnam, by Watergate, by inflation and unemployment, and they were asking two questions: Could our government be made to work again? and Could it be a source of pride again? The public-opinion polls, he declared, said that a majority of Americans thought the answer to both questions was no. But Carter, coming down boldly on the side of the angels, said he believed the answer was yes.

He closed with a story about Admiral Hyman Rickover, his one-time boss in the navy, whom he pictured as the ultimate no-nonsense commander: "All the time I worked for him, he never said a decent word to me." In their first interview, Carter said, Rickover had asked if he had always done his best as a midshipman at Annapolis.

"I wanted to say yes," Carter recalled, "but I thought of all the times I'd read a novel or listened to classical records when I should have been studying. So I had to say, 'No sir, I didn't.'"

Whereupon, Carter said, Rickover glared at him scornfully and demanded, "Why not the best?"

That, Carter concluded—and by then the room was hushed—was the question America must ask itself in 1976: *Why not the best?*

It was corny and self-serving, but it worked. The Kiwanians leaped to their feet, applauding. I too was moved. Perhaps all of us, cynical novelists and God-fearing Kiwanians alike, sometimes wish we had always been our best. Carter had touched his audience not with "issues" but by tapping into emotions that were universal.

The candidate on ERA

The next day, beside a swimming pool at a Holiday Inn in Clearwater, the leader of a group of schoolgirls asked Carter's position on the Equal Rights Amendment.

Carter grinned. "I can answer that in three words. I'm for it."

He might have stopped there. The schoolgirls were cheering and Jody Powell was signaling that it was time to go. But Carter had more to say:

"I come from a part of Georgia where almost every woman worked.

My mother was a nurse. My wife's father died when she was thirteen and her mother became a seamstress, making clothes for the more prosperous women in town. I've seen women working in southern textile mills in a way that shamed and embarrassed me. I've worked in the fields, and I've never seen men work as hard as those women. We tried to pass ERA when I was governor and we failed. And do you know who our main opponents were? The John Birch Society and the textile mills!"

If that digression was more for my sake than the schoolgirls, it succeeded. Minutes later, as we drove to the airport, I was so bold (not to say unprofessional) as to compliment his ERA remarks. Carter frowned. "Half those people probably oppose ERA," he said impatiently.

The candidate at home

We arrived at Carter's home in Plains about seven that evening. Amy ran out to greet him. She was nearing eight then.

"What did one wall say to the other wall?" she cried.

"Meet you at the corner!" he called back, and scooped her into his arms.

Rosalynn greeted us and soon the two of them were deep in conversation about his trip, the crowds, the money raised, and so on. After a minute or two, Amy was literally jumping up and down in a vain effort to gain her father's attention. Embarrassed, I struck up a conversation with her. I said I had a daughter her age whose favorite book was *Charlotte's Web*, and I asked if she'd read it.

"Yes, and I've read *Stuart Little* and *Trumpet of the Swan*, too," she informed me.

Little lady, I thought, you are *all right* on E. B. White.

Carter left and returned a few minutes later, barefoot, wearing jeans and a polo shirt. It was almost dusk and the skies were overcast. "Come on," he said, "I'll show you our town."

We got into his Oldsmobile and for nearly an hour he drove me around Plains, pointing out milestones from his past. "That's our church. . . . That's the housing project where Rosalynn and I lived when we came back from the navy. Our apartment cost $31 a month. . . . That's the school I attended. . . . That's my uncle's worm farm—he ships worms all over the world. . . . That's the cornfield where I used to play baseball. We had seven whites and three blacks on our team. . . . That's the house where I grew up; Daddy sold it while I was in the navy. . . . This is the house we built for my mother while she was away in the Peace Corps."

He stopped beside a peanut field. We got out, and he pulled up a plant and told me more than I ever expected to learn about the growth of peanuts. He broke open a peanut and we shared the meat. As we drove back to his house it started to rain. "You can see why they called it Plains," he said. "It's so flat that the water doesn't have any place to drain to."

After we pulled into his driveway, we stayed in the car while he talked a little longer. "We built this house in 1961. I figured it up once; it's the fifteenth house Rosalynn and I have lived in, counting the navy." He started to get out, then turned back to me. "There's just one more house I want to live in. Then I'll settle down here for good."

The candidate's wife

Rosalynn had put Amy to bed, and the three of us had dinner at the Carters' little breakfast table. Afterward, Carter said I might want to talk with Rosalynn, and he excused himself. The first thing I'd noticed about her was how pretty she was, with her high cheekbones, her dark, slightly slanted eyes, and her enigmatic smile. She's seemed shy at first, but once her husband was gone she spoke passionately, as if she'd been waiting a long time to tell someone her story. I recalled something Hamilton Jordan, the campaign manager, had said to me in Atlanta: "She wants to be first lady as bad as he wants to be president." He laughed. "Hell, she wants it worse than he does."

Rosalynn told me about her husband's first race, for the state senate in 1962: "We had a new cotton gin. That's why he won. He'd been all over the district telling farmers about our cotton gin. But I think he'd been planning to run for a long time."

She recalled his 1966 race for governor: "It hurt to lose. The idea that Lester Maddox would beat Jimmy—I couldn't believe it. Kids would tease our son Jack. You know, they'd say, '*Les-ter Mad-dox beat your dad-dy, Les-ter Mad-dox beat your dad-dy.*'"

Rosalynn gave me a far more candid account than Carter had of how they suffered for supporting the integration of their church: "It was tough. People wouldn't speak to us in church. But we were willing to take the consequences. Here's the kind of thing that happened. We went on a vacation trip to Mexico in 1965. A rumor started that we were at an integration camp in Alabama. It was right in the peanut season—that's how we make our money. But when we came home we didn't have any customers. There was this one man who liked us. He said, 'Jimmy, nobody's gonna bring you peanuts; we found out about you and that integration camp.' We had to track down the story to the man who started it and prove it wasn't true.

"Jimmy was the school board chairman. We'd always had terrible schools. Jimmy had a plan to consolidate, but everyone just said he wanted to integrate the schools. That was one time we got boycotted. Jimmy just wanted to *help* the schools. It was after his plan got beat that he decided to run for the state senate."

I asked why she thought her husband was running for president. She was startled, as if I'd asked why the sky was blue. "I don't know why he does it. I guess he just thinks it's right. Jimmy has strong feelings about things. He won't let anybody push him around. He appears kind of meek or something. People always underestimate him. Nobody thought he could be elected governor. I never thought why he did it. I guess he just has strong convictions."

I asked about her role in her husband's campaigns.

"For four years before he was elected governor, Jimmy campaigned almost every day. He'd leave on Monday and come back on Saturday. He'd drive himself. While he was driving he'd put the names of people he'd met on a tape recorder and I'd write letters to them. Later on I traveled too. I don't think anybody's ever campaigned harder than we have. We know what a campaign is. Sometimes the drive from Atlanta to Plains was the only time we'd have alone together. I'd tell him the hard questions I'd been asked and he'd tell me the answers to give. I'd be at a factory gate every morning. I couldn't have done it if I thought it'd never stop. But you want to win and you know that's what you've got to do.

"I'd make five or six speeches a day. Once I was on television and someone asked me, 'Mrs. Carter, where do you go from here?' Well, I didn't know where I was, much less where I was going, so all I could think to say was, 'I think I'll just stay here a few days.'"

The candidate's dirty mouth

The next morning we went to Carter's peanut warehouse and I met his soon-to-be-famous brother. My notes say: "Billy—a good ole boy—a round, happy face—wearing boots and a T-shirt with 'Billy' on it. Billy talks about the rain, JC about the new campaign-finance ruling." Carter showed me around the warehouse, then we returned to his home. While he went through his mail, I looked at his scrapbooks and asked an occasional question. Speaking of the openness he would bring to government, he declared that if one of his Cabinet members wasn't candid with Congress, "I'd fire his ass!"

In midmorning, Carter's son Chip and his wife, Caron, came to drive me to Americus, where I would catch a bus back to Atlanta. Carter and I had said our good-byes, but as I was getting into Chip's car he came running after me.

"Could I ask you one favor?" He seemed embarrassed.

"Sure."

"What I said about the Cabinet member. That I'd fire his ass. Could you put that off the record?"

I vowed to protect the candidate from his dirty mouth. It probably wasn't fit to print anyway.

I returned home and began to write my piece. It was an important one to the Carter camp, and Jody called on the afternoon of September 11 to ask about my progress. I confessed I'd done no work at all that day, because that morning Ann had given birth to our son, Michael Patrick.

My article on Carter turned out to be very favorable. If he had not always been the soul of charm, he had always been interesting. I admired his role as an outsider and his liberalism on many issues; if he was not the perfect liberal, he was probably as liberal as he could be and still have a chance of being elected president. I probably underestimated the extent to which his liberal talk in Florida was tactical—he had to court the left, because he wasn't going to woo the right away from George Wallace—but he'd still spoken out boldly when he might have waffled.

I opened the story with the "blonde at the bar" incident and followed with his dramatic remarks about the women working in textile mills and the fight for the ERA. Those scenes, and his efforts to integrate his church in Plains, were sure to endear him to the Eastern liberals for whom reading the Sunday New York *Times* is a religious experience. In the months ahead, many of Carter's supporters told me it was my piece that turned them on to his campaign.

I wrote that Carter "may or may not become President, but he is certainly one of the more interesting men to seek that office in recent times. His career suggests complexity, with its progression from farm boy to naval officer/nuclear scientist to peanut farmer/politician. Personally, Carter is a soft-spoken, thoughtful, likable man, an introspective man who enjoys the songs of Bob Dylan, the poems of Dylan Thomas. . . . Yet this slightly built, seemingly shy man is also one of the most driven, relentless, downright stubborn political campaigners who ever came out of the South."

Hamilton Jordan had outlined for me the scenario that they believed would gain Carter the nomination: win the Iowa caucuses in January and the New Hampshire primary in February, beat Wallace in Florida in March, and use those victories to gain the money and publicity needed to win the big-state primaries later in the spring. They assumed the convention would not deadlock and therefore would not nominate a noncandidate like Hubert Humphrey or Ted Kennedy. They believed the party would reject Senators Henry Jackson and Lloyd Bentsen as too conservative, and the race would come down to Carter against a liberal, possibly Representative Morris Udall.

That made sense to me, and I wrote, "Carter's scenario does not seem as preposterous at the end of 1975 as it did at the beginning. He has progressed to being a frontrunner for the Vice Presidential nomination and a serious candidate for the Presidential nomination." In fact, the scenario unfolded to near-perfection during the next year.

I didn't say much bad about Carter. I thought my job was to introduce him—the debunking would come soon enough. I noted only that his critics said he was motivated by "rudderless ambition," that he'd courted the segregationist vote in his 1970 race for governor, that his speeches were sometimes dull, and that he "cheerfully put the knife" to George Wallace with veiled references to his health and finances.

I didn't use another example of how nicely Carter could wield a stiletto. The third or fourth time I heard him tell his Amy joke, I caught the zinger. Betty Ford had said she wouldn't be surprised *if* her teenage daughter had an affair. In Carter's account, the affair went from the hypothetical to the historical—from "if she had an affair" to "Mrs. Ford's remarks about her daughter's affair," a rather large leap to make if you're talking about someone else's daughter.

But I didn't use that, because I wasn't sure Carter knew what he was saying, even after he added vaguely, at one stop, "I think it's a mistake to encourage immorality."

"Carter's pitch is more idealistic than ideological," I wrote. "He says America is drifting, that people are ashamed of their government and that all he wants is to see America with a government 'as idealistic, as decent, as competent, as compassionate, as good as its people.' He closes almost every speech by saying earnestly that he would never tell a lie to be President—a piety that makes some journalists groan aloud, but that apparently impresses many listeners."

I'm glad I caught that, because not many reporters did, then or later. They thought his rhetoric was corny. It was, sometimes, but it was that rhetoric, and the political perception behind it, that made him president. Far more than his Washington-based opponents, Carter understood how disgusted Americans were with politicians, and not just with Republicans. Carter's rivals, being the object of that disgust, had a hard time understanding it.

Carter understood that America needed reassurance, needed a candidate who would talk of love and hold out the promise of healing. He was speaking a different language than his rivals, and if they and the media did not understand his language, that was their problem, not his.

John Lennon once said that by the time the Beatles began to make records their best music was already behind them. It may be that Carter's finest moments came during his long, lonely journey of 1975. I count myself lucky to have witnessed his early performance. In time, under the terrible pressures of a national campaign, he became a more conventional candidate. But that summer he was soaring. He had found his message, and the people were responding. No matter if the crowds were small; they would grow. Carter was in his glory; he truly did know something the rest of the political world didn't.

By mid-December, when the *New York Times Magazine* published my article—with a cover drawing of Carter as a country boy in straw hat and overalls—the campaign was far from my thoughts. Ann and I had taken Laura, just turned eight, and Michael, aged three months, to Key West for the holidays.

On New Year's Eve, Ann and I and my brother Mike, who'd driven over from Texas, had dinner on a terrace overlooking the ocean at a place called Louie's Back Yard. Around midnight, as fireworks exploded over the water, I suggested that we each predict the outcome of the presidential election, still ten months away.

Mike said Ford would beat Humphrey.

Ann said Kennedy would beat Ford.

But I, marching to a different drummer, predicted that Jimmy Carter would defeat Ronald Reagan.

I was close.

2
I JOIN THE CIRCUS

"I have good news, Patrick!"

"Well goddamn, man, out with it!"

The caller was Michael Korda, my editor at Simon & Schuster. The date was March 17, 1976, St. Patrick's Day, the day the paperback rights to my new novel, *The President's Mistress*, were auctioned off. Ann and I had spent the day none too calmly awaiting the results of the auction. The paperback rights to my three previous books had gone for $2,000, $12,500, and nothing. But the publishing houses had of late engaged in bidding wars that brought six-figure bonanzas to lucky writers. And thanks to the success of the Woodward-Bernstein books on Watergate (and the herd mentality of publishers), Washington books were "hot."

Michael told me the amount of the sale. I scribbled it down for Ann to see: $250,000.

She turned away. It had been a long wait. Then we broke out the champagne.

I called some friends to share my good news. I might have rung up Air France and reserved tickets for Paris. Instead, I called Peter Bourne and Mary King and said that if Jimmy Carter needed a speechwriter, I was available.

Carter did not immediately accept my offer. He was already in negotiations with Bob Shrum, who had written for Senator George McGovern in 1972, and who joined the campaign in April. He only stayed nine days, however, whereupon he resigned and wrote a magazine article warning America that Jimmy Carter was *not a real liberal*.

Precisely!

After the Shrum fiasco, Carter wanted no more speechwriters, but then he lost some primaries to Governor Jerry Brown of California. He was still the frontrunner but the people around him were starting to sweat. Could the nomination slip away, after all they'd been through? The only thing they knew to change was Carter's rhetoric. The candidate was perfectly content to go on giving the same speech, declaring that he would never tell a lie and sought only a government as good as the American people, but his top advisers believed he needed a new writer, whether he wanted one or not.

Thus, Jody called on May 11 and asked if I was still interested in writing for Carter. I agreed to meet him that night at the Washington Hilton, where Carter was speaking at a fund-raising dinner. Before I left, I told Ann that if they offered me the job I'd have to take it. Why? For the challenge. Because, after my paperback sale, I was on a roll, eager for a new adventure. And this: My first book, *The Presidents' Men*, was about the White House staffs from FDR to LBJ. It focused on such bright young men as Harry Hopkins, Clark Clifford, Ted Sorensen, and Bill Moyers. There's a touch of Walter Mitty in every writer; now was my chance to see if I could perform in the arena, not just scribble on the sidelines.

I knew there could be problems. I'd been my own boss for a long time and didn't like anyone telling me what to do. Yet my book's success perhaps had solved that problem. I could work for Carter because I didn't have to work for him. My book had given me independence, what politicians call "fuck-you money."

I found Jody in the hotel lobby, surrounded as always by reporters. We escaped to the bar and I got to the point:

"Look, not to be coy, I'll do it."

"That's great."

"And don't worry about money. If it works out, I'll go on the payroll later."

"That'd be good," Jody said. "We're sorta in a bind until the matching funds come through."

I leaned forward. "I wish you'd tell me what the hell I'm stepping into."

Jody gave a tight little grin. "You're stepping into a vacuum," he said.

Later, after Carter's speech, Jody and I fell in beside him. "Pat's coming aboard," Jody said.

"Good deal," the candidate said, and shook my hand. I would learn that he could go days without saying more than "Good deal" and "I understand" to his staff. Each was intended to end the conversation.

We crowded into an elevator. "I hope I can do you some good, governor," I said awkwardly.

Carter flashed his famous grin. "We'll have fun," he promised, and he was a man who never told lies.

Two mornings later I joined the campaign in New York, where Carter was speaking to some scientists at the United Nations. I said hello to Ted Sorensen, who was an informal adviser to Carter, and to Milt Gwirtzman, a Washington lawyer who'd been traveling with him as an unpaid issues adviser. They introduced me to Zbigniew Brzezinski, a Columbia professor who advised Carter on foreign policy. Zbig gave me his card.

As we chatted, an inner voice kept asking me, "*What the hell are you doing here?*" Sorensen had been Jack Kennedy's alter ego. Gwirtzman was a longtime Kennedy adviser. I, by contrast, had never been in a national campaign and was vastly uninformed on the issues in this one.

I didn't know that both Sorensen and Gwirtzman had tried unsuccessfully to write for Carter. What I thought were my weaknesses would prove to be my strengths. I hadn't written speeches, but I could write, and that was what mattered. And it was just as well that this was my first campaign. Your first campaign, I came to understand, is like your first love: pure passion, something you give all that's in you. Men who come back a second or third time have lost that innocence; they tend to be old whores, out to turn a trick or make a buck. Nor was my innocence of national issues necessarily a problem: Shrum was a whiz on the issues and he had lasted barely a week.

Even the fact that I barely knew Carter was not a handicap. Later I realized that if I'd known him better I wouldn't have written for him as well.

That first day, in New York and later in Detroit, I spent my time watching Carter, taking notes on what he said, looking for ideas for speeches. During a meeting he had with Jewish leaders in Detroit, my eyes fell on a woman in her forties. She at first seemed bored and vaguely unhappy, but as Carter spoke she took on a look of wonder, as if she'd never heard a politician talk about love and compassion before, as if he gave her something to believe in. It was an entirely subjective impression, but it stayed with me and soon helped inspire my first important speech for Carter.

On the next morning's flight to Washington, I sat with Milt Gwirtzman, whom I'd known around Washington since the early sixties. Milt was a wry, soft-spoken, doleful looking man who sported one of the world's least-convincing hairpieces. He began our talk by praising *The President's Mistress*, a good way to deal with any writer. It developed that of all the people who speculated on the identity of my title character, Milt was the only one to realize she was suggested by a woman we'd both known in the sixties who'd had an affair not with a president but with a celebrated presidential assistant.

Jody joined us and we discussed what Carter might say that day to make news. The candidate was not part of the discussion. Jody had already warned me that he wouldn't ask us for ideas; it was up to us to propose them.

Our issues conference consisted of Jody and Milt skimming the New York *Times* for ideas. Happily, that morning's edition carried an editorial criticizing President Ford for postponing the signing of a U.S.-Soviet agreement to limit underground nuclear tests. Clearly, Ford wanted to delay the deal until after the Michigan primary, lest his rival, Ronald Reagan, use it as evidence that Jerry Ford had gone soft on the Ruskies.

The *Times* deplored the fact that U.S. foreign policy was thus hostage to politics—and we decided to deplore it too. I started drafting a statement, borrowing generously from the *Times*, and continued to work on it after we landed and were driving to a rally in Oxon Hill, Maryland. While Carter spoke, I called Zbig Brzezinski and he ticked off more examples of Ford's waffling. I finished my draft, Jody read it, and we jumped into the back seat of the candidate's limo as it left the rally.

"Pat's got the foreign-policy statement," Jody said.

I handed Carter my two-page draft. He slipped on his glasses and began to read. I waited anxiously.

"Why didn't you type it in capitals?" he demanded.

I had no answer to that, but Jody confessed that he'd neglected to tell me to use caps.

"It makes it easier to read in a car," Carter explained.

Carter cut one of Zbig's examples of Ford's waffling and added his own example. Then he frowned.

"Why did you say that twice?"

He showed me what he meant: I'd repeated that it was time for the Democrats to unite behind one candidate. I confessed that I'd had no good reason to make the point twice—it was a case of sheer incompetence.

Aside from that, Carter liked the statement. We charged that Ford's foreign policy "has become hostage to Republican party politics" and that "the Ford administration is paralyzed by political timidity."

With the statement agreed upon, we talked for the rest of the ride into Washington, where Carter would meet with AFL-CIO president George Meany. As we neared the AFL-CIO building, across Lafayette Park from the White House, Jody recalled Meany's past hostility to Carter.

"Times change," I ventured.

"Nothing has changed," the candidate said drily.

We arrived at eleven. Carter went off to meet with Meany, and I had an hour to get the foreign-policy statement typed and reproduced. I appealed to one of the union's PR men for a typewriter and copying machine.

He looked stricken. "Okay," he said grimly. "Just don't tell anybody I did it." In George Meany's world, this was giving aid and comfort to the enemy. But I had fifty copies of the statement at noon. An hour later, Carter incorporated our statement into a speech in Rockville, Maryland, and that evening he was on the national news, using my words to lambaste the president.

"What a hell of a process!" I enthused that night. "You write it in the morning, he delivers it at noon, and it's on the evening news."

Milt Gwirtzman looked glum. "I've been writing stuff all these months, and it hasn't worked like that yet."

I would learn that the process did not often work like that for anyone.

I'd been thrilled to see Carter using my words to blast Ford. A more serious student of politics might have questioned our strategy. Did we want to attack Ford, and thus strengthen Reagan's chances of becoming our fall opponent? (In retrospect, we should have been doing everything in our power to make Ford, not Reagan, our opponent—we should have been out strewing Jerry Ford's path with rose petals.) Moreover, our immediate problem wasn't Ford, but beating Jerry Brown in Maryland.

My own instinct—and clearly Carter and Jody agreed—was that denouncing the president on the evening news was by definition good. Moreover, I *liked* blasting Jerry Ford. When I left for the campaign my friend Joe Goulden gave me a copy of his book on Harry Truman's 1948 "give-'em-hell" campaign. That was my idea of a campaign: to give the Republicans unshirted hell.

What I didn't understand was that I was injecting myself into one of the most delicate and complex issues facing our campaign. Call it the High Road/Low Road issue. I liked to write tough speeches, Carter liked to deliver them, and the media liked to report them. The problem was that give-'em-hell speeches were not necessarily compatible with the smiling, Sunday-school image that had been part of Carter's success. We felt that routine political rhetoric, when used by Carter, unfairly became news—Mr. Clean gets mean—but that wasn't likely to change. We never really resolved the question. I continued to write tough statements, he continued to deliver them, and the media continued to express shock that a good Baptist could be so lacking in Christian charity.

Greg Schneiders, who became my best friend on the staff, liked to joke that letting me write for Carter was like giving firewater to the Indians.

On Tuesday, Carter lost badly to Brown in Maryland and barely beat Udall in Michigan. On Wednesday I was holed up in the Castaways Hotel in Las Vegas, writing a speech for Carter to deliver the next day before the California state senate. Jody and I agreed that he needed a strong speech, if only because it was to be delivered on Jerry Brown's home turf and we all loathed California's boy governor by then.

The heart of my speech was an attempt to explain why Jimmy Carter was going to be president. All week I'd been talking to reporters who professed to be baffled by Carter's success. The man was *fuzzy on the issues*, they declared. It seemed blindingly clear to me that most Americans didn't give a damn about the traditional issues. The real issue was America's post-Vietnam, post-Watergate disillusion.

Carter believed that, of course, and presented himself not as an issues-oriented candidate (like Mo Udall, who never won a primary) but as a decent man who believed America could be great again. I remembered the woman in Detroit who'd seemed to gaze at Carter with a hunger to believe again, and I wrote:

"I think the political campaign this year is operating on two levels.

"On one level, we have the tangible issues—unemployment, welfare, taxation—but on another level we have the intangible issue of the cynicism and apathy that afflict too many of our fellow Americans.

"Our people have been through too much. They have been lied to and cheated and tricked and bullied and confused and ignored, and they have finally had enough.

"They are crying out, not for government that is liberal or conservative or ideologically pure, but just honest and effective and compassionate.

"If I had to sum up in one word what this campaign is all about, that word would be faith. The American people want to have faith in their government."

Carter delivered my speech before the California senate, and it bombed. The California solons, overwhelmingly pro-Brown, talked and wandered around as an angry Carter rushed through the text. The reporters ignored our "two levels" analysis; the day's news was Carter being heckled outside the state capitol. The only reporter who commented on my speechwriting debut was the ineffable Bob Novak, who called the speech a "fiasco" in the Evans-Novak column.

We flew to Reno for a big outdoor rally. Some young people were holding up an "Amnesty Now" banner; others jeered them. When Carter took questions he was quickly called upon to address the explosive amnesty issue.

He began by praising those who served in Vietnam.

"They didn't have enough money to hide in college so they went to Vietnam. They didn't want to go. They didn't know why they were there. They wanted to stay home but they went. About 50,000 of them were killed. Another hundreds of thousands came back, wounded in different ways. In my opinion they are the greatest unrecognized, unappreciated heroes this country has ever known. . . .

"I am a deeply moral person, I hope, and I know that if someone has a deep commitment against the war, they have a right to do as they choose. Many of our young people went to Sweden or Canada. I could never bring myself to declare amnesty, a blanket amnesty for those who defected from our government."

Opponents of amnesty began to applaud, but Carter held up his hands for quiet.

"Wait, wait, wait, wait. . . . The war has been going on now in Vietnam—it started about thirty years ago. A lot of those young people have been in Sweden or Canada for fifteen years. I think it's time the war was over. So the first week I'm in office as president, I'm going to declare a pardon for all those young people who defected. There is a subtle difference. I'm not going to emphasize it. To me amnesty means that what you did was right and you are to be congratulated for it. Pardon means that what you did, whether it was right or wrong, is forgiven. So I'm going to declare a pardon and forget the Vietnamese war and let those young people come home."

The crowd cheered and the people with the amnesty banner lowered it, as if to say they were satisfied. It seemed a moment of genuine reconciliation, a small miracle, right before our eyes. One might hope that as Carter's amnesty/pardon formulation had satisfied these few thousand people, it might soon satisfy millions, and help end the war's bitter legacy. Carter, if pressed, would admit that the meanings he gave amnesty and pardon were not those in the dictionary. They meant what he wanted them to mean, but he had resolved the conflict in his own mind and perhaps could resolve it for all America.

After the campaign, seven months and hundreds of speeches later, I asked Carter if he remembered the Reno rally. "Of course I remember it," he said.

We talked on the flight from Reno to San Francisco. I had to be in Waterford that weekend, because of long-standing plans, and I'd decided to stay home a few extra days to work on a conservation speech. In truth, I was discouraged by my first week on the campaign. I had scored one success, by rewriting a New York *Times* editorial, and produced one speech, based on my own brilliant political analysis, that was a disaster. No one seemed to care what I did, and I thought my most useful contribution might be a major issues speech. Given Carter's strong record on the environment, that seemed a good place to start.

Carter was annoyed by my plan.

"I want you to read over all that I've said about conservation," he told me. "I want anything you write to be consistent with what I've already said. You may think you can write better than I can, but I want this speech to use my words, not your words."

I said I hadn't intended to put words in his mouth, and I returned to my seat. I tried to understand his state of mind—it was hard for him to accept the idea of someone else writing for him—but I still thought he'd been needlessly rude.

Earlier that week, a young man from the issues staff had boarded the plane to brief Carter on some complex policy matter. We were talking when Greg Schneiders said Carter was ready to see him. The young man fell apart. "I can't do it," he cried. "I just can't talk to him. You explain it to him."

It was like the moment in a war movie when it's time to attack and one of the GIs is afraid to go over the top. The fellow was so petrified that I wound up briefing Carter on something I knew nothing about.

I wasn't afraid of Carter, but I was starting to see that to work for him was like riding an emotional rollercoaster. I flew home that night, spent a much-needed weekend with my family, and began to wonder if there was any graceful way out of this mess.

3
WE SEE AN AMERICA

I was home working on the environmental speech when Jody called on Wednesday morning.

The day before, Carter had won three southern primaries but lost three in the West. He was spread too thin; it looked as if the stop-Carter coalition of Mo Udall, Frank Church, and Jerry Brown might nibble him to pieces in the final primaries.

"We're in New York," Jody said. "You've got to come up. We've lost our theme. We've got to find something new to say."

I asked what he thought Carter should say. He didn't know, except that he wanted to blast the stop-Carter forces and show how Carter was different from them.

I packed quickly, glad to be returning to action; working at home on an environmental speech had seemed the height of irrelevance. By then I realized that in a campaign (to paraphrase what Ken Kesey told his Merry Pranksters) you're either on the plane or you're off the plane, and if you're off the plane you cease to exist. Jody's call had put me on the spot: If I had anything to contribute to this campaign, now was the time.

Soon, as I was driving my ten-year-old Buick convertible east on Route 7 toward Washington National, I was ablaze with ideas. I began scribbling phrases on a manila envelope that was beside me on the seat. Each phrase began "I see an America. . . . " I kept writing on the shuttle flight to New York, my ancient portable typewriter on my lap, and by the time my cab reached Manhattan I had a draft of a speech.

I met Jody at someone's office on Madison Avenue, typed a clean draft, and gave it to him with a note that said: "Here are some ideas and phrases that Governor Carter might play with. I think the important thing is that he move from any attack on the stop-Carter movement to a positive and passionate statement of his vision of the American future. This should be inspirational, Kennedyesque if you will, but I think it is what a lot of people are hoping for."

The speech started with a slap at the opposition:

"We have seen this campaign come full circle now, from 'Jimmy Who?' to 'Stop Carter!' The people who ignored me then are opposing me now, but mine is still the same campaign it was a year ago. . . .

"My critics don't want to stop Carter. They want to stop the reforms I am committed to. They want to stop the people of this country from regaining control of their government. They want to preserve the status quo, to preserve politics as usual, to maintain at all costs their own entrenched, unresponsive, bankrupt, irresponsible political power.

"I am running for president because I have a vision of a new America, a different America, a better America, and I do not think it is shared by those who are trying so hard to stop my campaign.

"I have a vision of an America that is, in Bob Dylan's phrase, busy being born.

"I see an America that is poised not only at the brink of a new century, but at the dawn of a new era of responsive, responsible government."

My "I see an America" litany went on to include honesty in government, fair taxes, full employment, quality education—everything but free love and nickel beer. Finally I concluded:

"This is my vision of America. It is one that reflects the deepest feelings of millions of people who have supported me this year. It is from them that I take my strength and my hope and my courage as I carry forth my campaign toward its ultimate success."

Jody liked the speech and that night we gave it to Carter, who slipped it into his pocket without comment. He spoke the next morning at an AFL-CIO convention in Cincinnati. Once again I waited anxiously to see if he would speak my golden words. Instead, he started telling the "Little Veteran" joke. A meek Little Veteran drops by his neighborhood bar for a glass of sarsaparilla, only to be taunted and beaten by a Big Bully. The first time the Bully knocks down the Veteran, he says, "That was a karate chop from Korea." The next time he knocks him down, he says, "That was jiu-jitsu from Japan." Finally the battered Little Veteran escapes, only to return a few minutes later with a paper bag under his arm. He abruptly knocks the Big Bully across the room and declares, "When he wakes up, tell him that was a tire tool from Western Auto."

That drew a big laugh from the unionists, but it set the national press corps abuzz: "That was a Wallace joke—didja hear?—that's an old Wallace joke." Clearly, Carter would be guilty of racism by association if he'd told one of George Wallace's jokes. I later checked with Carter, who said indignantly that the Little Veteran joke was indeed his but that Wallace liked it so much he'd asked permission to use it. Carter granted permission (a matter of professional courtesy here) and the Alabaman popularized the story during his presidential campaigns.

After the joke, Carter returned to his basic stump speech, and I assumed he either hadn't liked my material or didn't think it right for this audience. Then, abruptly, he began reading my statement. The reporters sitting around me woke up and began scribbling madly. The audience of fifteen hundred union officials quieted down, and when Carter finished, they gave him a standing ovation. Reporters surrounded me, demanding copies, which of course I didn't have. Some congratulated me; they were so sick of Carter's stump speech that anything new sounded like the Gettsyburg Address.

Then their mood changed. They began to focus on the paragraph that denounced his critics and their "bankrupt, irresponsible political power." The pack instinct took over. The story became "Carter attacks critics" instead of "Carter's new vision." Later, they demanded that Carter identify these venal but unnamed politicians. Humphrey? Jackson? Meany? Brown? I would have said "All of the above," but Carter backtracked, and finally said he was talking about the Republicans, which was ridiculous.

I was flabbergasted. Somehow, I'd sabotaged my own speech. To me, the blast at the opposition was throwaway stuff, served up to satisfy Jody, but only a preamble to the "I see an America" litany. Jody later told me he'd known the negative passages would make the news, but they needed to be said. If that was true, he and I were operating on different wavelengths. All I saw was another opportunity wasted.

A couple of reporters told me that although they hadn't used the "I see an America" material, they hoped we'd run it by again. I passed that on to Carter the next morning and suggested that I rework the material for use at a union rally in Akron later in the day. He reluctantly agreed.

My goals, as I wrote in the back of the press bus on the way to Akron, were to make the revised statement 100 percent positive and, at Jody's suggestion, to add a note of humility that had been missing from the first one.

My new opening said, among other things: "Our campaign has not been perfect. In retrospect, more time might have been given to this state or that issue. Sometimes, in the heat of political combat, harsh words are spoken or overstatements made." Then we proceeded to the vision of America.

I gave Carter the new draft only minutes before the union rally in Akron. He began with his standard remarks. Shot down again, I thought. Then, abruptly, he slipped my draft from his pocket and said, "Now I'm going to read you a statement my staff has prepared."

I almost went through the floor. What the hell was he *doing*? Later, I supposed that Carter's vow to never tell a lie made it hard for him to utter my words as his own; he felt he owed the voters a truth-in-oratory disclaimer.

Yet he read the speech well, the crowd cheered at the right moments, and the reporters perked up again. It looked as if America might soon learn of Jimmy Carter's new vision. Alas, it was not to be. After the speech the reporters asked Carter if by speaking of "overstatements" he was admitting he'd gone too far in criticizing his opponents on the previous day. He refused to concede the obvious. Then they asked whether Carter considered some TV spots Udall was using in Ohio to be unfair. Carter said they were, and that became the day's news.

"Your new vision just got shot down for the second straight day," the Washington *Post*'s Jules Witcover told me, with some amusement.

In truth, the new vision was fighting an unwinnable battle against media hostility. Earlier in the spring the story had been "Carter Emerges," but now it was "Carter Stumbles." Carter's "I'll never tell a lie" pledge had left reporters hellbent to prove otherwise. Those two days of traveling around Ohio on the press bus had been sheer agony; in that moveable madhouse, after every stop, the reporters played their tapes over and over, furiously seeking some inconsistency. Carter could have delivered the Sermon on the Mount and no one would have cared unless it contradicted what he'd said the day before.

There were moments of comic relief. ABC's Sam Donaldson had a routine that satirized the candidate's "a government as good as its people" speech. "What we need," Sam would roar, "is a government as filled with greed, with violence, with lust, with corruption, with incompetence as the American people! Jesus Christ, if we had a government as good as our people, this would be Italy!"

On our last day in Ohio, a story quoted Carter as saying, in what he thought was an off-the-record talk, "I'm glad I don't have to kiss Teddy Kennedy's ass to be president." Asked at a news conference if he'd said it, Carter laughed and called for the next question. The reporters liked that. One of them found a "Kiss My Ass" T-shirt, which they presented to the candidate at the end of the day. "Have a good weekend, governor," someone yelled, and everyone cheered as Carter held up the T-shirt with a big grin.

It was a nice moment, an upbeat ending to a hellish journey, but it didn't change the fact that my "new vision" had been left for dead somewhere outside of Akron.

I spent the Memorial Day weekend at home, thinking about Carter's June 1 speech at the dedication of a new wing of the Martin Luther King Hospital in Los Angeles. Somehow, I thought, this speech before a largely black audience should be the occasion of something special. Groping for ideas, I sought out copies of Dr. King's "I have a dream" speech and of Robert Kennedy's anguished remarks the night King was killed.

I began writing on our flight west and continued when we arrived in Sacramento. I awoke in the middle of the night and wrote for an hour before falling back into bed. I skipped breakfast and wrote in the back of the press bus while Carter shook hands with hardhats at a truck yard.

"Hey, Pat, whatcha doin' back there?" Midge Costanza called to me. She was the vice-mayor of Rochester, New York, a funny, feisty woman who'd been an early Carter supporter.

"Just sittin' in the back of the bus, writin' a speech about Martin Luther King," I called back.

That was only partly true. My body was on the bus, but my mind was elsewhere, deep into my own fantasy, savoring the sweet chaos that Bob Dylan once called "a head full of ideas that are driving me insane."

I finished the speech at noon and gave it to Carter. He made only one change: He deleted a critical reference to George Wallace. Essentially, the speech gave form to a number of points Carter had been making at random. It noted that he had grown up, as King had, in the segregated South. It paid tribute to his mother, as one who had challenged segregation, to Dr. King and others in the civil rights movement, and to the contributions of Presidents Kennedy and Johnson.

It said of Dr. King, "He was the man, more than any other of his generation, who gazed upon the great wall of segregation and saw that it could be destroyed by the power of love."[1]

It said that King had spoken out against the war in Vietnam, over the protests of some advisers, and then:

"In the spring of 1968, he went to Memphis to help the garbage workers get a decent wage, to help the men who did the dirtiest job for the lowest pay, and while he was there he was shot and killed.

"But his dream lives on."

I quoted Robert Kennedy's words on the night of Dr. King's death, then continued:

"We lost Martin Luther King.

"We lost Robert Kennedy.

"We lost the election that year to men who governed without love or laughter, to men who promised law and order and gave us crime and oppression.

"But the dream lived on."

The speech ended with the "I see an America" litany, but now it had a context; Carter's vision was presented as a continuation of the dream of social justice that had inspired the civil rights movement, Dr. King, the two slain Kennedys, and Lyndon Johnson. In effect, Carter was offering himself as the new keeper of the dream.

He delivered the speech at six that evening, outside the hospital, his hair tossed by the wind, squinting into the setting sun. I thought he raced through the speech, as if he still resented speaking someone else's words.

1. The entire text of this speech can be found in the Appendix.

After the speech, as we were heading back to the press bus, the reporters surrounded me and began singing "We Shall Overcome." I was furious—they were making fun of my finest moment. But soon I realized their
hazing was a compliment. The speech had worked. Charles Mohr wrote
in the New York *Times* that this was "one of the most moving speeches on
the American racial dilemma heard in a long time" and added that "an
almost physical wave of love seemed to pass from the black listeners to
Mr. Carter."

Other newspapers and news magazines also praised the speech. Ted
Sorensen called and said, "I thought that speech was, if you'll forgive a
rather feminine word, beautiful." (Praise from the master.) Our people in
Atlanta printed copies of the speech for distribution in black neighbor-
hoods, as well as black and white buttons with its closing words, "I ask
your help . . . You will always have mine."

I had done something right, but I hardly knew what, because I was
writing on the run, operating on instinct. Only in retrospect can I make
some sense of what was going on in my mind.

To me, Carter's most attractive quality was his idealism, and the question was how it could be best presented. He had an interesting mind—
open, curious, and creative—and he expressed himself in original ways,
but his natural style, as showcased in his stump speech, too often lapsed
into Sunday-school homilies. At best, he spoke with the beauty of simplicity; at worst, he sounded simpleminded. His most famous line, the vow
never to tell a lie, was clearly doing more harm than good by the time I
arrived.

Although I admired parts of Carter's stump speech, I thought the time
had come for him to reach out to a wider audience with a more formal,
more traditional rhetoric. He wasn't talking in living-rooms any more. He
needed to focus his idealism into a "vision" that would reassure and inspire
people. To me, that meant the Kennedy-Sorensen rhetoric of 1960–63—
not its contrapuntal excesses, but the simple eloquence of the American
University speech of June, 1963. Thus, my "I see an America" material
was explicitly Kennedyesque. And it worked, by silencing the media criticism that Carter couldn't deliver a decent speech and by bringing him into what might be called the rhetorical mainstream. It wasn't a matter of
changing Carter, but of translating his idealism from his somewhat Del-

phic natural style into more familiar patterns that a national audience might more easily embrace.

Sometimes I was taking ideas that Carter had expressed at random and giving them narrative form. Sometimes I was looking hard at Carter, trying to understand him and to define him in ways that would not have occurred to him but that he could recognize as valid. Carter and I were in many ways strange bedfellows, but insofar as we worked together effectively it was in large part because we were both moralists.

As far as I was concerned, we weren't running against genial, bumbling Jerry Ford, but against the dark legacy of Richard Nixon. In that sense, the Martin Luther King speech was a kind of morality play. Although mostly devoted to praise of Dr. King, its emotional peak comes in the passage quoted above that contrasts the deaths of Dr. King and Robert Kennedy with the unnamed men who won the election in 1968 and "governed without love or laughter . . . who promised law and order and gave us crime and oppression."

Like a lot of people, I had believed in the optimism and idealism of the Kennedy years, and like a lot of people I had been hurt by the war and the Nixon years. Now there was a chance that this decent, moderate southerner could put the country back on track. Carter spoke of love, and that was fine, but I wanted more. I wanted him to speak with the passion and eloquence that had inspired us fifteen long years before. Our idealism had been frozen for so long; we needed to be warmed, to be moved. That, instinctively, was what I was trying to provide.

Despite our shared loathing of Nixon, Carter may at first have viewed my rhetoric with mixed feelings, as when he warned the audience he was going to read something his staff had prepared. He resented using someone else's words. Deep in his heart, he probably thought Kennedyesque rhetoric was frivolous and possibly sinful, but he couldn't ignore the success of the King speech.

On the evening of Sunday, June 6, I watched at home as Carter delivered the "I see an America" litany on national television. Jody had given the speech to Jerry Rafshoon, the Atlanta advertising man who handled Carter's media, and Jerry had filmed a spot of Carter reading it, which was now being shown on all three networks on the eve of the all-important primaries in Ohio, California, and New Jersey. I was told that the spots cost $50,000 and that no candidate had ever before bought national TV time during the primaries. The fact that Carter, who was notoriously tight with a dollar, would spend that much reflected his and his advisers' fears that he might yet be denied the nomination.

Even I, the proud author, recognized what a strange event this was. One moment Americans were watching their favorite Western or sit-com, and then, with no warning or context, there appeared this exhausted southern politician describing an American Utopia that he claimed to see. Who knows; perhaps it helped.

On Tuesday, we flew from California back to Atlanta. Everyone was in a good mood. Win or lose, at least the primaries were over. During the flight, Carter and I stood at the front of the cabin and engaged in the longest, most informal talk we'd had up until then. I remarked on how enthusiastic the crowd had been the night before. "I have to be careful not to excite people," Carter said. "Once they start to push and shove, children can get hurt."

A reporter joined us and asked how Amy was. Carter hesitated, then said, "She cried the last time we left. When she had school during the days, and only spent nights with her grandmother, it was all right. But now that school is out she gets bored and lonely." I was impressed by his candor: It was a hard thing for a father to admit. My daughter cried, too, when I left.

Carter was headed for a Sea Island vacation. He said he wished he could take Rosalynn to the more remote and unspoiled Cumberland Island, but he had so many people traveling with him now, and he feared they'd do it harm.

We talked about the foreign policy speech I was working on. He asked me to call and read a copy to one of his advisers, adding, "Be sure to call at night, when it doesn't cost so much." I noted that we could have some fun whenever he was ready to go after Henry Kissinger. He grinned, but said he wasn't quite ready yet.

I mentioned that I'd brought him some books. "Great!" Carter said, obviously pleased. I imagined him forty years before, as a boy in Plains, when a new book was a big event in his life. One of my books for him was Joe Califano's *A Presidential Nation*. I'd known Joe when he was Lyndon Johnson's top domestic aide, and I'd been promoting him as someone Carter should meet. But I was meeting resistance from Carter's inner circle, who saw Califano as a threat to their own ambitions.

I gave Carter a new book on labor policy by Mark Raskin of the Institute for Policy Studies. "Do you know IPS?" I asked. "It's a left-wing think tank. They're usually ten years ahead of everybody else in Washington."

Carter grinned. "Maybe we can cut that down to five."

Finally I gave him my novel, *The President's Mistress*. He laughed when he saw my inscription: "For Jimmy Carter, who will learn from this book that Washington is even a worse place than he thought."

He asked if *People* magazine's recent report on my paperback sale was accurate. He discreetly did not mention the dollar amount. I confessed it was true, and he asked how the money was paid and taxed, and in general expressed delight at my good fortune. A few days later, the New York *Times* carried a picture of Rosalynn carrying *The President's Mistress* under her arm, on their vacation.

Soon thereafter a man called me, identified himself as a reporter for a major newspaper, and began quizzing me about my novel. Weren't the Carters embarrassed by all the sex in it, he demanded. I replied, quite accurately, that there wasn't enough sex in the book to embarrass my eight-year-old daughter, much less people as widely read as the Carters. When he persisted, I hung up. Later, one of the supermarket tabloids carried a feature based on our exchange.

Carter closed our talk with words of praise for me. He said no one else had ever written for him to his satisfaction. "You came in and turned the campaign around," he declared. He said he hoped I'd stay through the election, but added that he couldn't make any promises after that. I thanked him and said that was fine.

Carter won the Ohio primary that night, whereupon George Wallace released his delegates, Mayor Richard Daley added his endorsement, and the nomination was locked up. He told me some of the details the next Monday when I met him at La Guardia Airport and rode into the city with him. He glanced at the speech I'd brought—he later spoke off the cuff—and we talked for the rest of the way. Bill vanden Heuvel, our New York co-chairman, was with us. Carter was in a good mood, although he admitted he'd been "pissed off" at Jody for oversleeping, which had delayed the press bus and thus his flight. "I'd have left them behind if I could have," he grumbled.

I asked Carter if he'd been surprised at how quickly his opposition collapsed. He smiled and recalled that eventful night: "Wallace called about one and told me he was releasing his delegates to me. I didn't get to sleep until three, and I slept until five-thirty, then I woke up and lay in bed thinking. Finally I called [Charles] Kirbo and asked him to call Scoop Jackson, and as soon as it was late enough I called Mayor Daley. I said, 'Mr. Mayor, I want to ask you a favor. George Wallace is going to announce his support for me at eleven o'clock, your time, and I don't want him to endorse me all by himself.' Daley said, 'Jimmy, whatever you want me to say, I'll say.' So he agreed, and Scoop Jackson told Kirbo I could speak for him, and then I put on my jeans—so I wouldn't look too establishment—and went out to tell the press."

Wallace's endorsement, by itself, would have inspired stories that Carter owed his nomination to the symbol of southern racism. Even with the nomination assured, Carter had moved swiftly—literally overnight—to seize it on the most favorable terms.

Carter described his subsequent meeting with Wallace in Alabama. He quoted Wallace: "I told my people I wanted to beat you in North Carolina worse'n I ever wanted anything in my life." He added that he would have endorsed Carter sooner but he was afraid of being rebuffed. Carter stressed how cordial their meeting had been. "He said Cornelia was at the beach and kept saying she wanted to come back and see Jimmy, but he told her, 'Honey, if you come, he'll have to bring Rosalynn and it'll get too complicated. Me and Jimmy have been governors long enough to know how to handle this.'"

As we neared Manhattan, I mentioned that a certain governor was being promoted as his running mate. "He's too lazy to be vice president," Carter said scornfully. "He doesn't get to his office until nine and he spends all afternoon playing golf."

Bill vanden Heuvel, who was well-connected socially, said Jackie Onassis would like to meet him. "I don't see any point to it," Carter said. "I'll invite her to the White House when I'm president." That was his attitude toward most jet-setters and movie stars. Other candidates wanted the beautiful people around for glitter, but Carter thought they'd hurt him among the southern white conservatives who were the bedrock of his campaign.

I mentioned a line that Jim Wooten had attributed to him in a recent *New York Times Magazine* article. Carter had supposedly said of Richard Nixon, "I loathe the bastard, but I pray that his soul finds peace." That struck me as the ultimate Carter quote, but he was not amused.

"I didn't say that," he snapped. Then he backed off. "Well, I didn't say it to Wooten."

Our car became snarled in crosstown traffic, only a few blocks from the hotel where he was to speak. Horns honked, nothing moved, and Carter fidgeted impatiently.

"I trust you'll do something about the New York traffic when you're president," I quipped.

"The mayor of New York ought to do something about it." Glaring out at the traffic jam, he added grimly, "We're gonna be late. I'd rather take a lickin' than be late."

Suddenly, to the horror of the Secret Service, he jumped out of the car and trotted the rest of the way to his destination.

A woman once asked me to name the most important quality for a speech-writer. I thought a moment and replied, "Audacity, madam, audacity."

Sometimes people would ask, "How do you know what Carter wants to say?" The answer, of course, is that I *didn't* know what he wanted to say—except insofar as what he wanted to say was what he was already saying, which was what his top advisers wanted him to *stop* saying—but I knew what I wanted him to say. That was where the audacity came in.

I saw myself as a fairly typical New Deal liberal. Growing up a have-not in oil-rich Texas had left me with populist inclinations; then, in my early twenties, I received a political education as a reporter for the Nashville *Tennessean*, a strong liberal voice in those days, one that supported two great senators, Estes Kefauver and Albert Gore, as well as the TVA, civil rights, and Jack Kennedy for president in 1960.

Ann and I arrived in Washington in 1962; I was a writer on Robert Kennedy's staff and she worked for the Peace Corps. The world was simple then. We were the good guys, who would soon end racial injustice (then perceived as a southern problem), poverty, the arms race, and related affronts to Camelot.

Then came John Kennedy's assassination and Vietnam and Nixon. I joined the celebrated anti-war march on the Pentagon in 1967, and in 1972 Ann and I were McGovern delegates to the Virginia Democratic Convention. We worked hard that summer, knocking on doors and making phone calls. It ended with our pitiful little "victory party" on election night. We'd barely arrived when it was clear that Nixon was winning by a landslide. Ann cried on the way home. I took her hand and said, "Don't. We did all we could," and I vowed that next time around, if I had anything to do with it, it would be those sons of bitches on the other side whose wives would be crying.

Like a lot of survivors of the McGovern campaign, I was looking for a winner as 1976 neared. Then by chance I found myself working for Jimmy Carter, so I summoned my audacity and wrote my speeches about a better America, put all my anger and frustration and lingering idealism into them, and hoped they might do some good.

Soon after the final primaries, Carter held a senior staff meeting in Atlanta. Those present included Rosalynn, Jody and Hamilton, Jerry Rafshoon, Chip Carter, Stu Eizenstat, the issues director, Ben Brown, a young black who ran the minorities program, Landon Butler, Hamilton's able deputy, Bob Lipshutz, an Atlanta lawyer and friend of Carter's, and Charles Kirbo, Carter's close friend and guru. I'd interviewed the inscrutable Kirbo for an hour when working on my *Times Magazine* piece and not gotten anything worth quoting. He was an enigma, a big, white-haired, sleepy-eyed lawyer who was some sort of father figure to Carter.

Their relationship once moved me to verse:

> Here's to dear old Plains, Georgia,
> Where the peanut springs up from the sod,
> Where Kirbo speaks only to Carter
> And Carter speaks only to God.

Midway through the meeting, Jody admitted a photographer, an older man who quietly began snapping pictures.

"Who's he with?" Carter demanded.

"*Time*," Jody explained.

"I don't want him in here."

"Well . . . " Jody stammered. "I thought since we weren't discussing anything important . . . "

"I don't want him in here," Carter repeated. "I'll explain later."

Jody ushered the startled photographer out, then Carter said, "I don't want a picture in *Time* that shows my senior staff and has only one black and one woman, and her my wife."

Jerry Rafshoon broke the tension by remarking that at least there were plenty of Jews on hand.

One Sunday in June, Greg Schneiders and Marie Hartnett came out for dinner and a swim with Ann and me in Waterford. Greg was about thirty then, a solidly built man with horn-rimmed glasses, thick brown hair, a serious look, and a sardonic sense of humor.

Greg was very much a child of the sixties. After college, he'd owned and operated a couple of bars in Washington. The first was a success but the second failed, leaving him broke. Late in 1975 he signed on with the Carter campaign's Washington office, earning about a hundred dollars a week. It was about that time that Jody, who'd been Carter's only traveling companion for a year, said he could no longer handle both him and the media too. Greg was chosen to travel with them as Carter's personal aide. This is sometimes called "coat-holding" in the political world, but it often leads to greater things. Given proximity to Carter, Greg's intelligence, unflappable manner, and relative conservatism made him increasingly influential.

Greg had grown up in a Catholic family that often discussed political and theological issues at the dinner table. Greg broke with the religion but retained the habit of dispassionate analysis. We became friends in part because we could laugh at the madness around us. This set us apart from Jody, who was in too deep to see anything funny about the campaign.

Greg and I could disagree on politics and still be friends. Jody and I rarely if ever disagreed on politics but would increasingly clash simply because of our egos.

Marie was thin and pretty, one of the gentlest women I'd ever known. They'd met a few years earlier when Greg had hired her to work as a waitress in one of his bars while she completed her graduate work in speech therapy. That summer Marie ran the Carter headquarters in Plains, and she and Greg rented a small house outside Americus that became a haven for our circle of staff and reporters. Knowing Greg and Marie was one of the bright spots of the campaign.

June 23

This was the day of Carter's speech to the Foreign Policy Association. Now that he was assured of the nomination, the speech took on considerable importance. The peanut farmer had to show the Eastern Establishment that he spoke the language of realpolitik.

Zbig Brzezinski had written a draft that was circulated among Carter's other foreign-policy advisers, who included Averell Harriman, Cyrus Vance, George Ball, Sorensen, and Henry Owen. I discovered, as I talked to these men, that a good deal of infighting was in progress, since most of them aspired to high office. Most were cautious in their criticisms lest they offend Zbig, who had the candidate's ear and was regarded as a dangerous adversary. Only Sorensen blasted the speech. He said there was nothing in it that Nixon, Ford, or Kissinger couldn't agree with, and that if this was the best we could do, Carter shouldn't make a speech.

My own view was that Zbig's draft was too long, too narrow in scope, too hawkish in substance, and too pedestrian in style, but not beyond salvation. I toned down the hawkishness, added references to human rights and the need to lessen U.S. arms sales, and wrote a new political introduction. I said that Carter had been to the American people, had learned from them the kind of foreign policy they wanted—and here it was. I thought that was the proper tone to take. After Vietnam, I had little but scorn for the foreign-policy "experts" and I knew Carter agreed.

I went to see Zbig at Columbia with my draft. He was shocked at my revisions, but he was also smart enough to see that they improved the speech. We went through it line by line, arguing out words and phrases, until we had a draft we both could live with.

I sent our new draft to Carter in Plains, with a summary of the points in dispute among his advisers. He then added his personal touch, a reference to Henry Kissinger's "secretive 'Lone Ranger' foreign policy."

Neither Zbig nor I would have thought of that; we were too sophisticated. But it was the best line in the speech and inspired a wonderful Herblock cartoon of Kissinger as a dumpy Lone Ranger who's been tossed off a white horse labeled "world events."

As delivered, the speech was moderate, high-minded, and unexceptional. It was therefore a success—the New York *Times* said so. That was why Carter never delivered another foreign-policy speech in the campaign. Zbig was always pushing for one—he had his East-West speech and his North-South speech and God knows what else—but our consensus was that we had everything to lose and nothing to gain by an encore.

Zbig was not wildly popular. That spring, Hamilton told Bob Scheer that he would quit if Carter, after winning the election, were to appoint Cy Vance as secretary of state and Zbig as national-security adviser. Alas, Carter did and Hamilton didn't. But Zbig was useful. You could call him with a question and get a straight answer, and that was not true of all academics. Carter took him with a grain of salt. The morning of the foreign-policy speech we met in Carter's hotel room in New York. Zbig was going to brief reporters that morning on the hidden meanings of the speech, and Stu said Zbig was "embarrassed" to be doing the briefing. "Not so embarrassed that he refused to do it," Carter noted.

Carter was in his bedroom when Zbig arrived. He studied the placement of the chairs, then demanded, "Vere ess Jeemy seeting?" That was Zbig: He always knew where Jimmy was sitting and always elbowed his way very close to the throne.

June 28

The speechwriter, home for a visit, serves up breakfast to his nine-month-old son and (with a humble nod to e. e. cummings) is moved to verse:

michael
(two-toothed like oliver j. dragon
defiant like his parents
festooned with soggy cheerios
a smorgasbord of gerber's greatest hits)
grabs the spoon
laughs
and eats my heart with his beauty

June 29

While I worked at home, Carter flew to Milwaukee to address the National Conference of Mayors. He gave a so-so urban-policy speech that I'd rewritten from a draft by one of our issues people. It contained too many buzz words like "countercyclical assistance," but it included one paragraph I liked:

"I think we stand at a turning point in history. If, a hundred years from now, this nation's experiment in democracy has failed, I suspect that historians will trace that failure to our own era, when a process of decay began in our inner cities and was allowed to spread unchecked throughout our society. But I do not believe that must happen."

A week earlier, on my way to see Zbig at Columbia, I'd passed through Harlem for the first time in a decade. I'd forgotten how vast and terrible and profoundly depressing it was. What bullshit American politics is, I thought. No major politician, certainly not Carter, was proposing anything that would improve the Harlems of America in any significant way. So I added my paragraph about failure and decay to the speech, then closed on a note of optimism. I did not personally share that optimism, but the genre demanded it.

4
NEW YORK, NEW YORK

On the morning of Saturday, July 3, eleven days before Carter was to deliver his acceptance speech in Madison Square Garden, we met at his home for our first discussion of that all-important address.

I brought a draft that I'd written and that Jody and I had gone over the night before. It opened by saying 1976 was not a year of politics as usual but a year of change—our "change" theme. It spoke next of Carter's grass-roots campaign, the fact that he'd taken his case directly to the people. This was the "outsider" theme that had been basic to his success but that now would be endangered if, as the Democratic candidate, he was seen as just another politician.

I included the idea of the campaign working on two levels: traditional issues and trust in government. I included a tribute to the Democratic Party, with specific mention of Presidents Roosevelt, Truman, Kennedy, and Johnson. Carter had rarely if ever done this during the primaries because it ran contrary to the "outsider" theme, as well as to his own instincts, but I thought he had to honor the party when he accepted its nomination.

I included several paragraphs of criticism of President Ford. When Jody and I talked the night before, we focused on the question of how hard to hit Ford, the old High Road/Low Road issue. We settled on what we considered a middle road.

Next came a passage that began, "Our people have suffered too much and too long at the hands of a political and economic elite that has made decisions without being accountable for its mistakes."

For years, in public statements, Carter had expressed concern, even outrage, at the injustice of a powerful few making decisions for the powerless many. But he'd never used as tough a phrase as "a political and economic elite," and it would be heatedly debated in the days ahead.

I closed with the "I see an America" peroration. I thought my draft was a decent starting point, but as Carter gazed across his cluttered desk at me he seemed ill at ease. Instead of talking about the speech, he paid me some unexpected compliments. He said again how great the Martin Luther King speech had been and that I'd come in and turned the campaign around. Finally he eased into the speech. There were some good things in my draft, he said, but he wanted to write a draft of his own, and he wished I would call some people and seek ideas.

Finally I understood his unease. "Governor," I said, "this is your speech, not mine. I have no ego involvement. You just tell me what you want."

Carter beamed, and we got down to business. "Call some people," he said. "Call Henry Owen. Sorensen. Dick Gardner. Bob Lipshutz. Call anybody else you can think of. Call bright young people you know. Tell them we're looking for ideas. A phrase. A paragraph. No more than a page. Then give me their ideas and we'll use them. Read my old speeches, too, the ones from the governorship. Have you got that collection I told you about?"

The Georgia Archives had brought out a collection of his speeches as governor. He gave me one of the first copies and inscribed it, "To my good friend Pat Anderson, who has really improved my speeches!" (Dare I say that this generous inscription, to my ear, had a hollow ring?)

"I don't want to attack Ford," he continued. "People are sick of hearing one politician attack another. I want to be positive. Let's talk about creating a sense of unity, between the president and Congress, and between the government and the people. I want to say that my campaign started with nothing, and formed an alliance with the people, and I don't fear being president as long as I can keep my alliance with the people."

He chided me about misusing "we" and "they" in my draft. All candidates talk a lot about "the American people" and most of them say, "The American people want honesty, they want justice, they want leadership." Carter always said "we."

"I am one of the American people," he reminded me. It was a small point, yet absolutely basic to his campaign. A few weeks later, I suggested this point to Fritz Mondale, but he didn't get it and kept on saying "they."

Jody was in and out of our meeting, and eventually Rosalynn served sandwiches for lunch. While we ate, Carter mused about writers. "The thing Bob Shrum didn't like about me," he began. Then he corrected himself. "*One* of the things Shrum didn't like about me was that I always wanted to change the speeches he wrote for me." He grinned. "Pat's the only writer I ever met who didn't get his feelings hurt if I changed his material."

"Governor," I said, "if I want my speeches delivered exactly the way I write them, I can go out on the street corner and deliver them myself. But I don't think I'd draw much of a crowd."

That was good for a laugh, but of course to me the point wasn't how much he changed but how much he used, and I wasn't doing badly on that.

Rosalynn talked about her sons. "Jack always had his nose in a book. He was the best student. Chip was always climbing a tree or getting into something. And Jeff . . . you never knew *where* Jeff was."

"I met Jeff in Atlanta last year," I said. "He drove me to Kirbo's office in his little sports car. That was one of the most hair-raising rides of my life."

Fearful that I might have upset Rosalynn, I added, "Probably I was late for my appointment, and that's why he drove so fast."

Carter laughed. "You're too tactful, Pat. Jeff always drives like that."

I spent the afternoon in Carter's study calling people: Sorensen, Stu Eizenstat, Bob Lipshutz, Bill Moyers, Olin Robison, a friend of mine who was president of Middlebury College, Henry Owen, of the Brookings Institution, and others who couldn't be reached on the holiday weekend.

After a long talk with pollster Pat Caddell, I wrote Carter a memo that said in part:

Pat thinks important things to stress—as we have—are time for a change, your independence, Ford's lack of leadership, and the general sense of drift and moral decay. . . . Pat and I came up with a line that—while you may think it too tough—we both found irresistible. It would be something like: "The man who pardoned Richard Nixon cannot give this nation the political and moral leadership it must have in the next four years."

I think you ought to consider that one. It would drive the delegates wild, and might hang a tag on Ford that he would never be able to escape. (And it happens to be true.)

I reached Sorensen at his country home and he cautioned against eliminating all criticism of Ford. "After all," he said, "people do vote *against* candidates."

Sorensen and others wanted to call back the next day with specific language, so I stopped work about five and Jody gave me a ride back to Americus, the nearby town where most of the staff and press were staying at the Best Western Motel. I was spending the weekend with Jody at his mother's farm outside Vienna, about twenty-five miles from Americus.

Jody clearly had the hardest job in the campaign—to be caught between Jimmy Carter, with his instinct for evasion, and the relentless fault-finding of the national media is not a fate you would wish on your worst enemy—and he handled it as well as anyone could. He was smarter and better informed than most of the reporters he dealt with, and he did not suffer fools gladly. He had a nervous stutter, which I took to be a mechanism that kept him from blowing up at people who asked him inane questions. Or he would snap, "Pardon?" There was nothing wrong with Jody's hearing, but asked a really dumb question he would grimly force the reporter to repeat it. Jody's "Pardon?" was like a slap in the face.

Jody was the one who had sacrificed the most for Carter, the one who traveled with him, leaving his wife and daughter behind for weeks at a time. He always treated Carter with deference, yet he was the one who could sway him in a crisis. I thought Jody saw Carter totally without illusions, that he loved him sometimes and despaired of him sometimes but accepted that, for better or worse, he had cast his lot with him. Once I asked Jody if his daughter and Carter's daughter played together. He shook his head. "I try to avoid that. I don't believe in raising expectations that may not be fulfilled."

As we left Plains that evening, Jody said he'd invited some reporters to his mother's farm for a cookout, but the cookout was not to be. When we stopped at the Best Western, someone produced a football and Jody ran out for a long pass. He was wearing boots and jeans, and he managed to twist his ankle badly. Someone drove him to the hospital, and I took his pickup truck to his mother's home and told her and his wife, Nan, of the accident.

June Powell, Jody's mother, was a plump, white-haired, quite wonderful woman who'd taught school in Vienna for many years. She was one of the white teachers who stayed on when the schools were integrated. "That boy," she sighed. "I remember when he played ball in high school. He was the quarterback and he was always the last one up from the pile, all skinned and bleeding."

That morning, before we had gone to see Carter, Jody had driven me around the farm, telling me about his family history. The land had been in his family for two centuries and it meant a lot to him. I had Jody in mind a few weeks later when I wrote an op-ed piece for the New York *Times* in which I said that many people in the Carter campaign were motivated "by a regional pride that has its roots many generations in the past." My article was in response to a column in which Bill Safire compared Jody and Hamilton to Nixon's Bob Haldeman and John Erhlichman. Jody and Ham had their faults, but they weren't convicted felons.

I was glad I had that weekend with Jody, a chance to see him on his native ground. In time we had our share of differences. That was inevitable. Jody tended to dominate everyone around him, and I didn't want to be dominated. But whatever our conflicts I always considered him a man of great intelligence and strength and thought Carter was lucky to have him.

I spent the next day, July 4, America's 200th birthday, working in Carter's study. He was away, first at church, then delivering a speech.

Sorensen called with a quote from Sam Adams ("I ask no greater blessing than to share with you the common danger and the common glory") and a line about relying on "quiet strength" in foreign policy. I assumed Carter would like "quiet strength," since he would see it as a description of himself.

Olin Robison urged that Carter take the high road, address first principles, and declare that America's best is yet to come.

Carter returned just as I located Bill Moyers, who'd conducted an excellent PBS interview with him in the spring.

"Say hello to Bill Moyers," I told him. "He's down in Marshall with his parents—it's their fiftieth anniversary."

Carter took the phone and quite correctly raised a point that had escaped me: Moyers, as a practicing journalist who had just joined CBS, might not be comfortable offering advice to a presidential candidate. That proved to be the case, but the two of them had a good talk and Carter wished Bill's parents a happy anniversary.

Carter asked me to take the best ideas I'd obtained and insert them into the speech. I did, adding new thoughts of my own and some language from his collection of speeches. I had mixed feelings about this grab-bag approach. We turned up some good ideas and phrases, but the danger was that the speech would become a patchwork instead of an organic whole. Still, we were making progress, and I left him my draft and went home for a few days.

I returned on Friday, the day before we flew to New York. I stopped by Carter's house, and he said he was still working on the speech but if Jody and I would drop by that evening he'd have a draft to show us. We talked for a minute about the potential vice presidents who'd visited him that week for well-publicized interviews.

"Mondale's great, isn't he?" I ventured.

"He sure is. But he gave in too easily when I pushed him. I was a little mean in my questions and he gave too easily. Muskie was the best. He doesn't really want the job, so he didn't care."

At six that evening, Jody and I were leaving the Best Western. Jody had a rental car, which I was driving so he could read my draft on the way. He was still using a cane because of his twisted ankle. When a burly young man stepped in front of us in the parking lot, I took him for some local pal of Jody's and stopped the car.

"What can we do for you, friend?" I asked.

"That man over there wants his car back," the youth said ominously. Standing nearby was a short, husky, sour-faced man who proved to be a local car dealer. He claimed that the rent on the car was overdue. He was accompanied by his two sons, one of whom weighed at least three hundred pounds.

After a bit of discussion, Jody growled, "Give the son of a bitch his car back."

Soon he and the car dealer were nose to nose, and their exchange deteriorated to the level of "Don't call me a son of a bitch, you son of a bitch!"

Jody seemed willing, indeed anxious, to take on the car dealer. That left me to handle the two sons. I saw it all: We'd be beaten up and thrown in jail, and the acceptance speech would never be written.

Unburdened by South Georgia macho, I suggested that we all go our separate ways in peace, but my diplomacy failed. Jody and the car dealer continued to exchange blood-curdling threats—but somehow the first blow was never struck. Indeed, at one point Jody said, "You lay a hand on me and I'll swear out a peace warrant on you." That made me think I had misunderstood the encounter, that this was some strange Sumter County ritual in which mighty warriors exchanged insults but not blows.

Eventually we achieved peace with honor, surrendered the car, borrowed another, and proceeded to Plains, where Carter was delighted by Jody's account of the parking-lot showdown.

He gave us Xerox copies of his new draft, which was handwritten and ran twenty-five pages on yellow legal paper. He had added a declaration from his Georgia inaugural address that the test of a government wasn't its popularity with the powerful but how fairly it treated those who must depend on it. Also from that speech he'd added a line about the duty of government to make it easy for people to do good and hard for them to do evil.

Before the tribute to great Democrats, he'd added, "I have never met a Democratic president but I have always been a Democrat."

At my suggestion, as a personal touch, we added a description of how, when he was a boy, he and his family would sit around a radio connected to a car battery and listen to the Democratic conventions in far-off cities.

He added the biblical quotation "Ye shall know the truth, and the truth shall make you free."

He elaborated on my "political and economic elite" with a phrase about "unholy and self-perpetuating alliances between money and politics."

He'd kept the "I see an America" ending, but with a significant change. When I had first written that material six weeks before, while driving to the airport, I'd thought myself divinely inspired, like Paul on the road to Damascus. But our friend Bill Safire, in a recent column, had helpfully pointed out that "I see an America" had been used by a great many politicians, including his former boss, Richard Nixon. Safire delighted in comparing Carter to Nixon.

I told Carter he could either change the phrase, to avoid such criticism, or he could keep it and to hell with Safire. Carter changed it to "We can have an America," which I thought was OK because it sounded a bit less visionary and more pragmatic.

In sum, there was a lot of pure Carter in his new draft—and that, I thought, was what the process was all about—but it was also rough, disorganized, and badly in need of work. That was my job, and he told me to proceed.

The next day, Saturday, July 10, as we flew to New York, I gave Carter some remarks for the rally that awaited us outside the Americana Hotel. He read my draft, then wrote his own in longhand, retaining only these sentences of mine: "We have lived through a time of torment. Now we approach a time of healing." I was glad he'd liked "a time of torment"—it was the title of one of I. F. Stone's books—and I added it to the acceptance speech.

I worked on the speech that night and the next morning in my room on the twentieth floor of the Americana. Carter was in a princely suite one floor above me. I had a call that morning from Adam Walinsky, a lawyer who'd worked for Robert Kennedy. He said he had some ideas about the speech and that Landon Butler, Hamilton's deputy, had suggested he give them to me. Because of my respect for Butler, I invited Walinsky up to my room. Stu Eizenstat and Pat Caddell also wanted to talk about the speech, so I invited them as well.

Stu and Pat made an odd couple. Stu, our issues director, was thin and balding, soft-spoken and self-effacing, highly intelligent, and dedicated to liberal ideals and to Jimmy Carter as their vehicle. Pat, our pollster, was big and fleshy, fast-talking and self-serving, and dedicated mostly to his own boy-wonder mystique. I viewed him as a world-class bullshit artist, but the candidate was mesmerized by his polls and the mumbo jumbo he conjured up from them.

Walinsky was a dapper, self-confident man of about my age who launched an interminable lecture on everything we southerners didn't know about the ethnic/Catholic/working-class voter. He said we must focus on the working class, not minorities; we must stress family stability and traditional values; we must quote Al Smith and/or John Kennedy and/or the Pope; we must be against crime and for home ownership, et cetera, et cetera, et cetera. Walinsky was blessed with what a professor of mine used to call a firm grasp on the obvious, and his lecture would have been more welcome if it had lasted ten minutes instead of two hours. I was starting to keep an Audacity File, and Walinsky's filibuster was clearly a contender for my grand prize. Later he surpassed himself by sending the candidate a thirty-page, single-spaced memo on the same subject.

When Greg Schneiders called and said Carter wanted my new draft that night, not the next day, I broke up the meeting.

I made a few changes based on Walinsky's advice. I also softened the "political and economic elite" section. Our group had agreed this was necessary. Even I, who'd come up with the phrase, was worried about it. The "elite" became "a small group of people," and the line about them sending their children to "exclusive private schools" became sending their children "elsewhere."

I wrote a cover memo to Carter that said in part:

I have tried to make the improvements I thought called for without doing violence to your draft.

However, a long talk I had this afternoon with Stu, Pat Caddell, and Adam Walinsky led to some substantive additions. Essentially, we agreed there was a need to make a more specific appeal to the concerns of working-class Catholics. You will see a number of fairly obvious appeals: the addition of the JFK quote and the Al Smith tribute, the talk of traditional values, the reference to the Democratic party helping the immigrants, etc.

As Stu's attached memo indicates, he and the rest of us are still fascinated by the "man who pardoned Richard Nixon" line. Jody argues that you are absolutely committed to not raising that issue. We all agree that someone else should say it if you don't.

Stu felt strongly that we should reinstate the assurance on Israel.

There was a long discussion of the "power elite" section. Most of us agreed it was a little too strong. This version is toned down.

Jody and I felt the strong statement on peace should be added.

In general, I think this is a good draft, but can still be tightened.

I took my new draft to Carter at nine, and he said he'd try to read it that night. Then I escaped to a nearby restaurant with Greg and Marie. During dinner, Greg said, "You know, I think Jimmy was just expecting some comments in the margin, not a new draft."

What could you say? If you a hire a writer there is always the danger that he will write.

After I returned to my room, Milt Gwirtzman came and asked if he could see the speech. I gave him a copy of the latest draft and he said he'd slip it under my door after he'd read it. Then, finally, I went to bed. I hadn't mentioned it to anyone, but that long Sunday of speechwriting had been my fortieth birthday.

The next morning, Gwirtzman hadn't returned the speech, so I went to his room and picked it up. When I asked what he thought of it, he said, "Not bad," without enthusiasm.

In a memo to Carter that morning, I noted that the speech lacked any slogan like "New Deal" or "New Frontier" and listed various suggestions people had made—"A New Vision," "A New Future," and the like. I passed these along because so many people had urged me to, but I doubted that Carter would be interested. He thought they were gimmicks. I agreed, and admired him for rejecting them.

I also chewed over the "economic and political elite" again: "I fear it will raise questions and cause concerns that will hurt you more than it helps you. . . . As Stu's memo pointed out, it sounds a bit like a conspiracy theory. I guess that's why I pressed you on whether you could be specific, could name some. I think it would be better if you said 'the bureaucrats, the politicians, the corporate executives who have great control over our lives.' I think you should give this section—and the potential problems involved—serious thought."

There were certain ironies in this exchange. One was that I, having coined the phrase, was backing off. In my book *The Presidents' Men*, I rather disdainfully called Ted Sorensen "one of the most cautious liberals who ever lived." Now I was learning how the pressure of events (and fear of the media) makes everyone cautious. It was perhaps ironic, too, that a novelist, innocent of national politics, would presume to advise a veteran politician on such a matter. But everyone around Carter knew his weakness for explosive phrases. It was, I think, a form of verbal showing off.

We'd seen it in the furor over "ethnic purity" and we would see it again before election day. It was the flip side of his eloquence; he was like a jazz musician who, reaching for high notes, will sometimes hit a very sour one.

Ann arrived at noon on Monday. A few weeks earlier, when it had become obvious that Rosalynn needed her own press secretary, I'd urged her to talk to our friend Mary Hoyt. Mary had worked with Ann in the Peace Corps public-information office, and she'd been Eleanor McGovern's press secretary in 1972. Rosalynn hired Mary, who then asked Ann to help her at the convention.

Ann and I caught a cab over to the *Newsweek* offices for a luncheon Kay Graham was giving. Such notables as Ben Bradlee, Carl Bernstein, Nora Ephron, and Theodore White were on hand, but the real head-turner was Lauren Bacall. "Doesn't she look *wonderful?*" people kept whispering.

I chatted with Theodore White, a famously nice man who had been a hawk on Vietnam. Seven years before, I had reviewed his book on the 1968 presidential campaign on the front page of the *New York Times Book Review* and given him a rough going over. Recently we'd been introduced on the press bus. He shook my hand, perhaps reluctantly, and said, "Yes, I believe I remember your name." I said, "Mr. White, the war is over," and our dealings were pleasant after that.

Back at our hotel, I ran into Stu Eizenstat, who asked me to come to his room to discuss the speech. Pat Caddell and Milt Gwirtzman joined us. Gwirtzman said he had some criticism from Ted Sorensen and Ted Van Dyk, a tall, mournful-looking fellow who was known as an adviser to Hubert Humphrey.

"How did Sorensen and Van Dyk get involved?" I asked.

"Oh, anytime you give a speech to me you're giving it to Sorensen and Van Dyk," Gwirtzman explained.

I glanced at Van Dyk's marginal notations, which revealed an uncanny ability to disapprove of Carter's favorite lines. He wanted to cut our Bob Dylan quote, presumably because Dylan was too radical.

When our meeting broke up, I found Jody and we went to see Carter. "I haven't had a chance to read your draft," the candidate said. "Greg's got me overscheduled."

Greg's view was that Carter agreed to meet with countless politicians, then blamed him for it. In any event, Carter had Greg cancel several meetings the next day so he could work on the speech. He said he would discuss it with several of us at 5 P.M.

That evening, Ann and I went to an early dinner at a little French restaurant with Greg and Marie and Marty Schram, then *Newsday*'s Washington bureau chief. Greg told me with some amusement that Gwirtzman had told him that Sorensen thought the speech was "not presidential," and we should start over from scratch.

I was not amused. I'd seen Sorensen twice that day, and neither time had he mentioned reading the speech, much less not liking it. The irony was that both Sorensen and Gwirtzman had tried to write for Carter and failed, because they were still writing for Jack Kennedy. When they said Carter's prose wasn't presidential they meant he wasn't the right president.

Later that evening, Ann and I went to Madison Square Garden to hear Barbara Jordan's keynote speech, then caught a cab uptown to the *Rolling Stone* party.

Jann Wenner had invited twice as many people as his townhouse would hold, and before the evening was over there were two parties, one inside and one out on the street. As we fought our way up the steps, Ron Kovic, who'd lost the use of his legs in Vietnam, was being denied admission, and he was not taking it well. "That's right, you sons of bitches, throw me down the stairs," he roared, as we inched past. "I'll bite you on your fucking ankles!"

Inside, I ran into Sy Hersh. That spring I'd foolishly told an interviewer that the crazed investigative reporter in *The President's Mistress* might be a little like Sy. "*You son of a bitch!*" he roared from across the room. "*I thought that was Bernstein!*"

I spoke with Tom Hayden, whom I'd met a decade earlier when I was on a magazine assignment and he was in Newark organizing poor people for SDS. We talked about ways he might contribute to our campaign, but in truth I doubted that Hamilton would want an alliance with Tom. That proved to be the case. Quoting Bob Dylan was about as radical as we got.

Gwirtzman called the next morning and asked if I'd seen Walinsky's draft of the acceptance speech. I had, thanks to Greg. Walinsky had written his version on behalf of the Kennedy caucus, using mine as a framework but adding new language and ideas. I said I'd found its style too ornate and its substance too conventionally liberal for Carter.

"Oh, I think it's good," Milt said. He asked how our draft was progressing.

"Fine," I said. "He'll work on it today. I think he's getting what he wants."

"Pat," Milt said gravely, "this speech is too important to be determined by what Jimmy Carter wants."

And there you had it. These people thought Carter was some hillbilly who had blundered into the nomination but couldn't possibly be elected, much less govern, without their brilliant advice. (Gwirtzman even suggested that Carter not have an acceptance speech, since even if we wrote him a good one he wouldn't know how to deliver it. He suggested that the acceptance speech be replaced by some informal means of communication, perhaps a roundtable interview with reporters.)

I thought I understood Carter better, not just his style but the process we were engaged in. Carter would move at his own pace. Most of all, he wanted this speech to be his, not mine or theirs or anybody else's. And he had a way of getting what he wanted.

The rest of Tuesday was hectic. Reporters kept calling, as did people with last-minute suggestions. Midge Costanza sought my advice on her seconding speech, and Congressmen Pete Rodino sent an aide for ideas on his own speech. Stu stopped by with a strange tale. Someone had told him of meeting a young delegate who claimed to have read Carter's acceptance speech and who, moreover, was telling people it was terrible. Stu had the young man's card: he was a minor official of a small southern town. All this made no sense. I'd shown the speech to no one except our top people and Gwirtzman. And Stu was quick to say that Milt wouldn't have shown the speech to anyone as irrelevant as this young man. For the time being the errant speech draft remained a mystery.

That afternoon I met the gag writers.

Their names were John Barrett and Jack Kaplan, and at Jerry Rafshoon's invitation they'd flown from Los Angeles to provide jokes for Carter's acceptance speech. The problem was that no one would talk to them. They couldn't get near Carter, Rafshoon couldn't be found, and I'd been putting them off for two days. Finally I said I'd give them five minutes. They hurried to my room, two very unhappy gagsters, and handed me two sheets of legal paper with four or five jokes written in longhand. I glanced at the jokes, thanked their authors, and hustled them out the door.

Then it was five o'clock, time for our meeting with Carter in his suite.

We gathered around a coffee table. Carter was in high spirits, perhaps because he'd been working on the speech all afternoon rather than greeting politicians. He wore slacks and a dress shirt with the collar open and the sleeves rolled up. He sat on a sofa with his son Chip on his left. Jody was next in the circle, wearing a vest and tie, but with his coat off and sleeves rolled up. I was next, in a chair opposite Carter, tieless as usual, my notebook on my lap. Pat Caddell was next to me, then Jerry Rafshoon, tieless and rumpled, on Carter's right. Greg was in and out, sometimes joining in the discussion, sometimes fielding calls.

Carter gave each of us a copy of his new draft of the speech. "I'm going to read this through aloud," he said. "I want you to interrupt me anytime you have a comment or criticism."

He had never before invited such criticism on a speech, and it proved that he understood how supremely important this one was. As a candidate, for eighteen months, he had made countless speeches, first to ten or twenty people in someone's living room, then to rallies that thousands attended; but now, only once, he would address the entire nation, tens of millions of voters who would be seeing him for the first time in more than a news bite. You could blow your inaugural—you were safely elected by then—but you couldn't blow the acceptance speech without risking disaster.

He began to read, slowly and carefully, and soon we were caught up in debate.

An early section of the speech paid tribute to candidate Al Smith, as well as Roosevelt, Truman, Kennedy, and Johnson. I'd included Smith as part of our wooing of Catholics, but that raised problems if we left out other defeated candidates like Humphrey, Stevenson, and McGovern, who had their constituencies too.

We chewed over that one—to cut Smith or add the others—until I said, "Smith lost. Why don't we just leave out all the losers?"

Carter grinned. "Now you're talking my language," he said, and that was it for Al Smith.

As Carter read his draft, I admired the editing he had done on my version. I had called Harry Truman "a fighting Democrat who showed us that a common man could be an uncommon leader, who told the timid that if they couldn't take the heat they should stay out of the kitchen." Carter quite correctly cut the overworked "stay out of the kitchen" and kept the better "common man/uncommon leader" phrase.

He used a paragraph from Walinsky about the Democratic Party being built "out of the sweatshops of the old lower East Side, out of the dark mills of Massachusetts," but he relocated the dark mills in New Hampshire, whose primary he had won, rather than the Kennedys' Massachusetts.

Our most heated debate was over the passage about "the economic and political elite who have shaped decisions and never had to account for mistakes."

"Who is this elite?" Rafshoon demanded.

Carter said it probably included prosperous Atlanta ad-men like Rafshoon.

Others protested that the passage sounded radical, or as if Carter believed in an elitist conspiracy. I said nothing. I had previously toned down the language, and he had restored it, so I assumed his mind was made up.

"I have a strong visceral feeling about that section," Carter said, and that was that.

We reached two sentences Carter had written in the margin. The first was, "The poor, the weak, the aged, the afflicted will be treated with respect and compassion and with love." As if that thought had inspired another, he continued, "I have spoken many times about love, but love must be aggressively translated into justice."

I said that the line about translating love into justice was wonderful.

"It ought to be," Carter said. "It's Niebuhr."

But it was Niebuhr filtered through Carter, and I felt that finally, in his own way, Carter was getting his speech.

Carter had added a line about "unholy, self-perpetuating alliances between money and power" that cheat average Americans. He brushed aside protests that "unholy" sounded pious and might revive the "religion issue," noting that "unholy alliance" was a common phrase and he could not be faulted for using it.

There were objections to his saying that government should make it easy for people to do good and difficult for them to do evil. Pat Caddell protested that "evil" sounded pious.

"Pat's got a guilty conscience," Carter joked. "He was out doing evil with Warren Beatty last night."

I said the line was vague: How would government help us do good? But Carter overruled me. The "do good/do evil" line was from his Georgia inaugural and it obviously meant something important to him, whether or not it meant anything to the rest of us. He did agree to change "do evil" to the milder "do wrong."

Carter accused me of an unexpected sin: a too-grand vocabulary. "You've said here, 'The first nation to dedicate itself explicitly to certain principles," he said. "'Explicitly' is too fancy. I want to use words that people down in Plains will understand."

"We could make it, 'to dedicate itself so clearly,'" I suggested humbly.

"That's the idea," Carter said.

Then he urged business, government, and labor to "discern the mutuality" of their interests. "Governor," I said, "I'm not sure the fellows at Billy's gas station will know what 'discern the mutuality' means."

Carter frowned, but agreed to a change. Soon I ousted "implacable" with the same Billy's-gas-station argument. One might question whether the level of national political discourse should be set at Billy's gas station, but I was having fun.

He had added a line about the immigrants who came to America having been "the best and the bravest."

"But they weren't," someone objected. "A lot of them were crooks and misfits and failures."

Carter was amused. "Well, you go tell Peter Rodino that his father was a crook," he said, speaking of the Italian-American congressman who would second his nomination.

Rafshoon raised a question about the "We can have an America" ending. Just before the acceptance speech, we'd be showing a film that ended with a voice-over of the "I see an America" litany. Could we use the material twice, or must we change the ending of the speech?

"You've got to keep that ending," I declared. "It's too good to lose."

Carter smiled. "Well, you are a little prejudiced on the subject, aren't you?"

Reason prevailed.

Our meeting broke up around seven with everyone in a good mood: We thought we had a winner. Carter was amused by our objections that "evil" and "unholy" might revive the religion "issue."

"Do you know what's the most religious thing in the speech?" he asked. "When I say 'brothers and sisters' at the end. 'Once again, as brothers and sisters, our hearts will swell with pride to call ourselves Americans.'"

As I was leaving, I handed Carter the two pages of jokes the gag writers had given me. He glanced at them without much interest. I still had work to do; I'd promised to give him some inserts for the speech that night.

One the way to my room I ran into Andy Young, whom I'd met for the first time that day, and asked the young civil rights leader to come read the speech. When he finished I asked what he thought. Andy looked uneasy. "You know, I'm not a very critical person."

"Come on, we want your advice."

"Well, this line about 'a return to the work ethic.' That sounds awful puritanical to me. Most folks work pretty hard already."

"I'll pass that on. What else?"

"I don't like the biblical quotation—'Ye shall know the truth,' that one. It doesn't seem to fit."

Those were his only criticisms, and to get those had been like pulling teeth. I wondered how someone so decent could survive in politics. We talked about the seconding speech he was to make for Carter the next night. Andy seemed overly modest about it, and the next day I sent him a note urging him to remember that he was a leader of a great movement, a symbol to millions of people, and he should speak out forcefully for his beliefs, as well as for Carter, when he had his moment before the nation.

I returned to Carter's suite at ten and found him with Rosalynn and Chip, watching the convention on television. I gave him my new material and told him about Andy Young's suggestions. He said he would rise at six the next morning and work on the speech, and asked me to come by at 8:45.

Carter was working at the dining room table when I arrived the next morning. He'd made the two cuts Andy Young suggested and decided to use two of the jokes that Kaplan and Barrett had submitted. One, playing off the Bicentennial, said Democrats were only united every two hundred years, and the other was that we Democrats were ready to take on the Republican Party—whichever Republican Party they put up. Both sounded pretty dim to me, but when he delivered them the delegates went crazy.

I took his draft back to my room and began typing my final suggestions. I urged that he insert "We will pray for peace and we will work for peace, until we have removed from all nations the threat of nuclear destruction."

His draft spoke of taking his campaign "to homes and shopping centers, factory shift lines and colleges." I urged him to expand the list, because I thought there was poetry in that litany of his long march to Madison Square Garden. He added "to barber shops and beauty parlors, to farmers' markets and union halls."

I persuaded him to change "*the* political and economic elite" to "*a* political and economic elite," which seemed a shade less menacing.

I was alarmed by one change he'd made overnight. We'd agreed that he needed a tough call for equal justice and against the double standard for rich and poor. "Make it mean," Carter told me, for this was how we would indirectly raise the issue of Ford's pardon of Nixon. I'd given him an insert that was neither mean nor notably inspired: "It is time for our government leaders to respect the law no less than the humblest citizen, so we can end the double standard of justice in America."

He had added: "I see no reason why big-shot crooks should go to country clubs and poor ones go to jail."

I loved "big-shot crooks," which (like the Lone Ranger foreign policy) reflected his genius for popularizing his ideas.

But "*go to country clubs*"?

It was classic Carter, at once both brilliant and off the wall. I said in my memo that I wasn't sure what he meant. If he was echoing the old right-wing notion that minimum security prisons were country clubs, I disagreed. Or did he mean literally that America's country clubs were filled with unindicted felons? I thought they probably were, but I didn't think he should say so in his acceptance speech.

I urged him to change the line to the unambiguous "I see no reason why big-shot crooks should go free and poor ones go to jail." He did, and it became perhaps the most popular and most quoted line in the speech.

After giving Carter my memo, I spent most of Wednesday in my room, available if he needed me, and meanwhile fielding calls from reporters and from people with some urgent idea for the speech. There were endless calls from women wanting a plug for the ERA, Jews seeking more homage to Israel, eco-freaks demanding a new manifesto, and so on. I thought one of the strengths of the speech was that he had resisted the pressures to turn it into a laundry list. He once told me if you started that you never stopped. At his best, that was how Carter campaigned: addressing America, not as a collection of special interests, but as one people united by shared concerns and values.

Jim Wooten of the New York *Times* called that afternoon. I'd only met Jim that week, but I knew him to be one of their best writers and also a very droll, likable man. He went right to the point: "I heard that Carter wrote a terrible first draft of the acceptance speech and nobody had the guts to tell him until Jody finally did. Anything to that?"

His question scared me. If the *Times* carried a story the next morning, the day of the speech, suggesting that it was a disaster, a lot of people would assume it was true, and other reporters might take up the cry. That kind of build-up could kill the speech before it was ever delivered.

"There's absolutely no truth to that," I told him. "Carter didn't write a bad draft and Jody didn't tell him he did."

I hesitated. Even if Jim believed me, the question was whether he would go with the story anyway. Plenty of reporters would have, and my denial wouldn't have helped much.

"Listen, Jim, I think I know where that story came from, because there are people on the fringes of this campaign who think they're smarter than Carter or his staff. But if you'll check with Jody or Greg or Caddell or anyone who was directly involved, they'll tell you the same thing I have."

"One more question," he said. "It is true that Adam Walinsky contributed a draft?"

"Yes."

"Did it become a major part of the speech?"

"Hell, no! We used two paragraphs."

"Okay, thanks."

"Look, have I knocked this down?"

"Yeah, you've knocked it down," Wooten drawled, being himself an Alabama boy. "But I'd like to come by tomorrow and talk about how the speech got written."

"No problem," I sighed. "No problem."

The next morning Carter announced that Senator Mondale would be his running mate, and there was a meeting in his suite of the candidates and their senior staffs. When I was introduced to Mondale, he gave me a copy of his acceptance speech, which he said he'd written himself, and asked me to read it for criticisms or possible conflicts with Carter's. I found his speech to be routine partisan stuff, but I didn't say so. I respected Mondale and didn't want to start our relationship by criticizing his speech. Things were too delicate for that. You felt the tension behind the smiles and hand-shakes, as Mondale and his people waited to see how they'd be treated by Carter and his people.

Instead, I made three minor suggestions: that he add a line about Carter having "gone to the people," that he add an anti-skyjacking declaration we hadn't been able to fit into Carter's speech (it would win Mondale his biggest ovation), and that he cut FDR's well-known line about the sins of the warmhearted, since several speakers had already used it. In the next issue of the *New Yorker*, Richard Rovere praised Mondale's wit and intel-lect but complained that neither quality "could be deduced from his ac-ceptance speech, much of which had been drafted by Carter's writers so that it could be delivered by anyone the nominee chose."

I met Ann and some friends for lunch at 21. It was a big day at 21—both Jackie Onassis and Ethel Kennedy were there—but my mind was on the speech. Had Carter finally stopped tinkering with it? Was someone typing it? Would we have advance copies in time? Politics has a way of spoiling everything else for you.

Around five, when copies were ready, I hand-delivered one to the *Times*, to help them meet their first deadline and to repay Wooten's trust in me. Then Ann and I went to Madison Square Garden and I gave a copy to Bill Moyers in the CBS booth high above the hall. Moyers and his colleague Eric Sevareid hurriedly read the speech while Ann and I watched the convention on one of their monitors.

After a while Sevareid rejoined us and gravely said, "Smorgasbord!"

"I beg your pardon?" I thought perhaps he was inviting us to dinner.

"Smorgasbord," he repeated. "Something for everybody."

The celebrated commentator was giving us his verdict on the speech, not in my view an enlightened one. Bill Moyers, with his Baptist background, understood it better.

We stood in an aisle high above the convention floor and watched Carter deliver the speech. I groaned when, during our tribute to ethnic groups, he pronounced "Italian" as "Eye-talian" and earned some jeers. But otherwise I was delighted. I loved his surprise opening line: "My name is Jimmy Carter, and I'm still running for president." The two gagmen had suggested it, as a joking update of his standard opening line when he was an obscure candidate. It hadn't impressed me, but Carter had seen that it could work.

As soon as he finished, I grabbed Ann's hand and made a quick exit. We therefore missed the scene when Carter and civil-rights leaders led the crowd in singing "We Shall Overcome." A lovely moment, but by then my wife and I were drinking champagne in a dark, sleek, quite excellent restaurant called Orsini's, no doubt surrounded by Republicans.

The mystery of the missing speech draft was solved the next evening. A rich and exceedingly stupid young southerner had invited the Carter staff for drinks at 21. Ann and I went by before meeting Greg and Marie, Pat Caddell, Warren Beatty, Michelle Philips, and some others for dinner. Our host at 21 proved to be the mystery delegate. He explained that he had been on duty at the Xerox machine the previous Sunday night, when I had given Gwirtzman a copy of the speech. In the wee hours Gwirtzman and Van Dyk asked him to run off some copies, he said, and he'd asked if he could make one for himself. He was alarmed to hear them talking about how dreadful the speech was.

The young man was soon in a state of panic. How could he save Jimmy Carter from delivering a bad acceptance speech? He began showing it to people for their advice. One of the people he showed it to, he said, was Orville Freeman, the former governor of Minnesota. The entire episode was incredible. There was not much news at the convention, and if this fool had put the draft in a reporter's hands, or had started a story that there was a fight over the speech, we could have had a disaster.

My response was not to return calls from Gwirtzman and Sorensen for several weeks. When Gwirtzman finally reached me, I blew up. "Dammit," I roared, "I saw Sorensen twice and he never said a word about not liking the speech, not a word, and then you people tried to go behind my back to Carter."

"You don't understand," Gwirtzman explained patiently. "That's how discreet Ted is. If he doesn't like a speech, he doesn't even tell the author."

The wonderful thing was, it didn't matter. The acceptance speech had been a success, despite everything. You could tell by what the papers said, by what people were saying, and soon by the polls. A couple of weeks later, when I arrived late at a staff meeting, Jody passed me a note on Caddell's report to the candidate: "According to Pat C. acceptance speech had tremendous positive impact. 'Perhaps greatest impact of any single speech in 20 years.' 78% favorable—16% unfavorable to speech. Thought you'd like to hear a good word now and then. JP."

Carter's acceptance speech had been his political zenith, and our convention had been his coronation, even as Reagan and Ford continued their bloody struggle for the Republican nomination. Carter held huge leads over them both in the polls. If he had packed up that night and flown home to Plains and gone fishing until election day, he might have won by a landslide.

Unfortunately, he campaigned.

5
EASY LIVING

The seven weeks between the convention and the official campaign kickoff on Labor Day were a good time, perhaps too good a time. In those easy summer days, the Republicans were in chaos, Carter was absurdly far ahead in the polls, and we staff and media people who were encamped at the Best Western Motel could divert ourselves with sex, drugs, gossip, softball, and other forms of innocent fun. The election seemed a mere formality, and a rather distant one at that.

On July 23, the Carter and Mondale staffs began a two-day get-acquainted meeting at the Sea Pines Plantation on Hilton Head Island, South Carolina, which is where rich southerners go when they die and sometimes before. Three scenes linger in the memory.

Hamilton

Hamilton Jordan presided over an opening session at which everyone was introduced. Our campaign manager, wearing a pair of too-tight tennis shorts, clearly relished his role as top dog; even Mondale deferred to him. Sometimes he would spice his introductions with a quip or barbed remark. When he introduced Tim Kraft, a field organizer with a reputation as a ladies' man, he drawled: "In the Carter campaign, we encourage our people to save on hotel bills by sleeping with our supporters, and this is the fellow who's slept with more supporters than anyone in history. It's got so bad that instead of a paycheck we send him another dose of penicillin every month."

Kraft, a swarthy young man with a Pancho Villa moustache, marched forward and replied: "Thanks a lot, Ham—you've been an inspiration to us all."

That drew a laugh, and it would have been funnier if Ham's wife hadn't been in the room.

When Hamilton introduced me, and I only waved, he said, "Stand up, Pat." I shrugged and stood up, whereupon he added, "Notice how well he obeys orders—that's why he's Jimmy's speechwriter."

Why did this smart, powerful young man behave like such an ass? Because he was insecure and/or a natural-born boor? Because, after the success of the acceptance speech, he thought I needed humbling? Because he wanted to impress a sweet young thing we'd all spotted on the Mondale staff? All of the above? There was an undercurrent of malice in the Carter world that I was only beginning to grasp. To understand it you had to understand the roles of the two most important men in the campaign, Jody and Ham.

It was possible to distinguish between them on a personal level—Jody's hair was light and Ham's was dark, and Jody was the more stable of the two—but politically they were indivisible. As long as they stuck together, they could rule Carter's world, Jody as Mr. Outside, managing the media, and Ham as Mr. Inside, controlling politics and patronage. They saw the people Carter didn't want to see and did the dirty work he didn't want to do. Carter was a military man and he believed in discipline, but it was not his job, as captain of the ship, to enforce it. He delegated that to Ham and Jody. To win their favor, via loyalty and humility, was to rise in Carter's world; to lose it was to twist slowly in the wind.

One of the first top campaign people to lose favor had been Peter Bourne, who arrived at Sea Pines a virtual pariah. Peter was not Jody and Ham's sort of guy—they were tough-talking South Georgia shitkickers and he was a tweedy intellectual with a flaky English accent. Moreover, his wife, Mary King, was the kind of hard-charging feminist they considered a royal pain in the ass.

Peter's downfall had begun a month earlier, when a long article in the Washington *Post* proclaimed him Carter's "closest friend" and added, "Peter Bourne was the first person to tell Jimmy Carter four years ago he should run for President."

Powell and Jordan happened to disagree with both of those points, and Bourne's star soon went into decline. Little items began to appear, vaguely attributed to "senior campaign aides," saying that Bourne was losing influence with Carter because he had become too fond of Georgetown cocktail parties or was seeking publicity for himself or whatever. Within a month Bourne was out as Carter's Washington spokesman, and was said to be writing a book.

I made a point of sitting with Peter and Mary at lunch, because I saw how many people avoided them. Not that it mattered. Before the year was out, many others would run afoul of the two overlords of Jimmy Carter's world, two young men who had reached levels of intellectual and emotional toughness that most human beings cannot imagine.

Mondale's men

After the staff meeting, Jody and Ham held a joint news conference with Jim Johnson and Dick Moe, Mondale's top aides. I was struck by the physical contrast between the Carter and Mondale men. Dick Moe and Jim Johnson were both tall and slender, wore horn-rimmed glasses and neat clothing, and looked as if they had attended Princeton, supported their local symphony, and were loving husbands and fathers.

And then there were Jody and Ham, looking like a couple of rawboned, narrow-eyed South Georgia thugs. There was always a hint of violence in them. I'd seen it in Jody's parking-lot encounter, and Bob Scheer captured it in *Playboy* when he described a time a car passed Jody too close and he roared "You fucking asshole!" and gave chase until his wife calmed him. One could not imagine the same scene involving Moe or Johnson.

The contrast extended to the candidates themselves. Fritz Mondale had thought about running for president, but Mondale was soft, and after he made a few swings around the country and saw how much mental and physical punishment was involved, he drew back. Carter accepted the punishment, and you can be sure that every time he looked at his vice president he reflected that Mondale was not the man he was.

There was this, of course: The Democratic party *had* put down too many roots in Harvard Yard and Georgetown, and it *did* need the toughness, anger, and obsessiveness the Georgians brought to it. But it was not a pretty sight when, from time to time, their capacity for violence turned inward, on our own people.

The good life

Charles Fraser, the developer of Sea Pines, took some of us for a cruise on his sailboat that night. The evening could not have been more perfect: a full moon, dazzling stars, a strong wind to speed us across the water. Most of the passengers gathered on the front deck, where Jody and Ham were holding court—"doing their good-ole-boy number," one woman called it—but I sat alone at the rear, nursing a beer, gazing at the distant lights of the resort, growing more and more depressed.

My mood was subjective and perhaps irrational. I knew that the Nixon staff, the Deans and Magruders and Zieglers, had come here in their years of power, and I imagined that Charles Fraser had taken them on this same moonlight cruise and that they had savored this taste of the good life just as we did. This crazy question kept buzzing in my ears as we sailed on through the night: "*What if we're no different from them?*"

In Plains the next Monday and Tuesday, Carter held the first of a series of briefings with experts in various fields. The visitors, celebrated men and women, aspiring Cabinet members, were brought the 120-odd miles from Atlanta in rented buses. Those big buses would groan and bounce the last half-mile down the narrow clay road to the Pond House, Carter's mother's house outside Plains, and then the passengers would emerge into the blistering Georgia heat and stumble the final hundred yards to the Pond House with terror in their eyes. Those arrivals looked like they had just completed the last lap of some hellish fraternity initiation in which the victims were professors instead of freshmen.

We had elaborate explanations of how much money we saved by bringing our guests down by bus instead of by plane, and how this gave them a wonderful opportunity to savor the scenic glories of South Georgia, but Carter surely knew that the television audience might see these arrivals as a certain humbling of the Eastern elite, and he could not have minded having that elite almost literally beat a path to his door.

Once his guests were inside, Carter would thank them effusively for coming (most of them would have killed to be there) and insist at length that he was the student and they were the teachers. After one such disclaimer, I scribbled in my notebook, "The more he protests his humility, the more he towers above them."

Yet Carter performed impressively. He never missed a beat in some long, complex discussions. He was not just there to learn, of course. He was studying men and women who might serve in his administration, and through them he was also sending a message to the universities and think tanks that he was no dummy.

The briefing on national defense was dominated by Paul Nitze, a well-known and formidable hawk who seemed to expect a Soviet nuclear strike within the hour. Confronted with Nitze's certitude, the others present, who included Cy Vance, Paul Warnke, and Harold Brown, rolled over and played dead rather than seem "soft." Amid the solemn discussions of MIRV missiles and second-strike capacities, one young lawyer twice urged the group to remember it was discussing the possible deaths of tens of millions of human beings. He was politely ignored.

Carter spoke boldly at the next day's economic briefing. The economists were gloomy about the future (with good cause, it turned out), and Carter kept telling them to give him a bold program of recovery, not piecemeal ideas. He said in part: "I made two thousand speeches while I was seeking the nomination and I know our people and I think the American people will go along with a four-year plan if they feel the president knows what he's doing. The country is ready for strong, bold moves, and political obstacles should not deter us from being bold."

He talked often of "the American people" that afternoon, as if he were already empowered to speak for them. I wondered if any candidate had ever been so confident three months before the election. He was on an incredible high.

He was also furious about the way one of the networks had treated him the previous day. Carter had gone out after the defense briefing and answered questions, and one reporter had focused on his saying "I don't know" a few times. "He made a joke of it," Carter said angrily, and suggested that Jody tell that reporter to "kiss my ass."

After the economic briefing, as we were all standing outside the Pond House, Jody mentioned to Carter that he was committed to deliver a certain speech the next week. Carter told Jody, loudly and angrily, that he had not agreed to that speech. This exchange took place near a cluster of reporters, some of whom were trying to record it. When Jody pointed this out, the candidate snapped that he didn't care.

Abruptly, Carter cooled down and asked Fritz Mondale, who was staying at the Pond House, if he wanted to have dinner with him and Rosalynn.

"Gee, Jimmy, I'd like to," Mondale replied, "but I've already asked my staff to have dinner with me here. We're going to grill some steaks."

Carter then surprised Jody, Greg, and me by inviting us to dinner.

Jody had to drive back to the Best Western to pick up his wife, Nan, and I caught a ride with Greg to Carter's house.

"Let's stop by Billy's station and get a six-pack," I suggested.

"I don't know if we ought to," said my cautious friend.

"Oh bullshit, Greg, I've drunk beer at Carter's house before."

"Yeah, but that was Chip's beer."

But we drove to Billy's gas station, where Billy and Chip and some friends were enjoying their happy hour along with a tall, handsome fellow who looked vaguely familiar. Chip introduced him as former Mayor John Lindsay of New York, who was there as a journalist. I shook Lindsay's hand, grabbed a six-pack, and got out of there. You didn't hang around Billy's station if you were invited to Jimmy's house.

But a problem arose at the candidate's house.

"I asked Greg and Jody and Pat to dinner," Carter explained to Rosalynn. "I thought we'd cook those steaks."

"Jimmy!" the lady of the house exclaimed. "I gave those steaks to Fritz Mondale."

"Oh," the candidate said glumly.

Life is a sit-com, I told Carter, but my humor escaped him.

Rosalynn retreated to the kitchen, eventually to report that, thanks to the good women of Plains, who brought endless casseroles and covered dishes to the Carter house, she had plenty to feed us.

Carter mixed a scotch and water and I opened a beer. Greg was off making phone calls, and Jody and Nan hadn't arrived yet. I brought up Carter's upcoming speech to the American Bar Association. He said he wanted a hard-hitting, populist speech, like his celebrated Law Day speech at the University of Georgia two years earlier. Gonzo journalist Hunter Thompson happened to be present for the Law Day speech, had been impressed by Carter's criticisms of the Georgia bar, and wrote glowingly of it in *Rolling Stone*, giving Carter unexpected cachet among some freaks, radicals, and serious drug abusers.

I wanted to know more about the Law Day speech. I had read the two handwritten poems that hung on the wall in his study. One, by Judy Carter, his son Jack's wife, expressed her pride and love as she watched him deliver the speech. The other was Carter's reply, saying that he drew his strength from his loved ones. I asked Carter if he had delivered the speech to shame the Georgia legal establishment for its failure to work for civil rights and social justice.

"It was more than that," he said. "Jack was a senior in law school then and I was concerned about him. In high school and college he'd been socially concerned, but I thought law school was making him more conventional, more conservative, and I wanted to tell him to see his law career as more than a way to make money."

"So your goal was to inspire your son, not to blast the lawyers?"

"Both," he assured me.

He didn't mention his other goal. The other Law Day speaker was Ted Kennedy; Hunter Thompson was present because of Kennedy, not because of an obscure southern governor. Carter, of course, had nothing but scorn—moral, intellectual, political, whatever—for Ted Kennedy, and after Kennedy's speech Carter discarded his original speech and scribbled notes for another, one that would put a great deal of moral, intellectual, and oratorical distance between him and the Massachusetts liberal.

He began: "I'm not qualified to talk to you about law, because in addition to being a peanut farmer, I'm an engineer and a nuclear physicist, not a lawyer. . . . Not having studied law, I've had to learn the hard way. . . . One of the sources for my understanding about the proper application of criminal justice and the system of equity is from reading Reinhold Niebuhr. . . . The other source of my understanding about what's right and wrong in this society is from a friend of mine, a poet named Bob Dylan."

He dropped the names of four of Dylan's songs before concluding, "So I came here speaking to you today about your subject with a base for my information founded on Reinhold Niebuhr and Bob Dylan."

Having thus impressed the man from *Rolling Stone*, and dumbfounded everyone else in the room, Carter proceeded to catalogue Georgia's failures in the area of social justice and to make clear that he was on the side of the angels and that the Georgia bar was pretty much on the other side. The major opposition to his ethics bill, he declared, had been lawyers. Lobbyists were charming fellows, he added, but they didn't give a damn about ordinary people. Doctors were fine people, too, but the AMA and its Georgia counterpart didn't care about the doctors' patients. In praising Martin Luther King, he mentioned that the slain civil-rights leader "was perhaps despised by many in this room." By the time Carter finished, it was possible to conclude that he was the only moral man at the Law Day ceremony, and perhaps in the entire state of Georgia.

Hunter Thompson's instincts were sound: Carter's Law Day speech—his relentless determination to upstage Kennedy—was fascinating, far more so than anything poor Kennedy was likely to say. (Kennedy's mention of his recent trip to Russia inspired Carter to relate that he'd first read *War and Peace* at the age of twelve; if Kennedy had said he'd been to China, Carter would have claimed to have invented gunpowder.) Yet if Carter's speech was fascinating, it was also pious and self-serving, inspired less by populist idealism than by his determination to outshine a politician he despised.

As we talked that evening, waiting for the other dinner guests to arrive, Carter thumbed through a collection of Niebuhr's essays. "His widow sent it to me," he explained. "One of my greatest regrets was not meeting Niebuhr before he died." He delivered a brief lecture on Niebuhr's role in modern theology, all wasted on me.

Jody and Nan arrived, and we all sat down to dinner in the dining room. It was a pleasant evening. The conversation centered on family and community affairs, with Jody and Carter doing most of the talking.

Carter expressed concern over the strain the tourist boom was putting on his church. He joked that at least the tourists doubled the collection most Sundays. He talked about his displeasure that many writers had pictured his mother as a liberal heroine and his father as a racist and reactionary. In truth, he said, his father had been the greater influence on his childhood.

Rosalynn spoke of her outrage when she discovered that someone had bulldozed the dogwood trees around the Carter family graveyard. Carter said he was unhappy because local officials had put up too large a sign at the graveyard.

Chip came in and asked if he could bring John Lindsay over. Carter frowned, Rosalynn shook her head once, and Lindsay stayed at Billy's station. Billy himself wandered in later, a beer in his hand and a tale on his lips. The tale concerned a reporter who had called Billy a liar.

"I said, 'Feller, you're 'bout to be *daid!*'" Billy reported, adding that the reporter had wisely withdrawn the insult. He told how he and Lindsay had drunk beer and taped an interview.

"I hope you were sober," Carter said with a smile.

"Well, I was when I started," Billy said.

I liked Billy. He had obvious limitations, but he was a very decent man, quite vulnerable beneath his bluster, and he was never unkind. Billy's visit that evening struck me as awkward. There was no invitation for him to sit down. He stood in the doorway, grinning and telling his stories, but I sensed a desperation behind his humor. Carter listened with what seemed a mixture of affection and impatience. When Billy left, I thought it must not be easy to be Jimmy Carter's brother. Or Jimmy Carter's child. Or Jimmy Carter's anything.

Carter commented during dinner that I could certainly use a haircut. Ho-ho-ho. Little barbs like that were part of his style. In that he contrasted with his wife, who was unfailingly pleasant. Rosalynn could be very tough and political, but her attitude toward the staff was uncomplicated: If you were helping elect Jimmy, you were her friend. Carter was more complex. He was compelled to put you down from time to time, just to remind you who was boss, or perhaps to remind himself.

We lingered over coffee. I began to suspect that Carter was ready for his guests to leave. I would have been. Around nine-thirty I suggested we go. I started to carry my plate to the kitchen, but Rosalynn wouldn't hear of it. Back at the Best Western, Jody and Greg hurried off to return calls and Nan and I went for a nightcap. She was an intelligent woman who had pursued her teaching career while Jody was off fighting the political wars.

"That was so strange tonight," she said.

"What?"

"Dinner. Jody has worked for Jimmy for six years and he's never asked us to dinner before. I guess when Mondale asked his staff to dinner, Jimmy thought he should too."

After we used Bob Dylan's line about "busy being born, not busy dying" in the acceptance speech, the New York *Times* published a letter from someone who said Carter had misquoted Dylan. We hadn't, although Dylan was referring to an individual and we used the line with reference to the nation, so I called the editor to protest. He said they'd been flooded with incoherent letters from irate Dylanologists and asked if I would write and set the record straight. I gladly did so. I've done many shameful things in my life, but causing my candidate to misquote Bob Dylan on national television is not among them.

At a staff meeting on August 2, Hamilton led a discussion of Carter's schedule for the next few weeks. One issue was whether he should address a labor rally in Detroit on Labor Day. "It's the traditional thing to do," Ham said, "but I'm not sure Jimmy should do the traditional thing."

I suggested that Carter kick off his campaign at Franklin Roosevelt's "Little White House" in Warm Springs, Georgia. Carter liked the idea, but no decision was made.

Jody said he wanted Carter to speak soon in the Midwest as a raid on the enemy heartland. Hamilton agreed, because that would show our man out campaigning and knock down the idea that he was overconfident.

Carter broke in to say that he didn't want to be overscheduled: "Let's don't let the darn thing degenerate so that we're out four or five days a week again."

The exchange reflected strategic uncertainty. As the Ford-Reagan battle raged on, Carter was presenting himself, by way of contrast, as the serene, self-confident candidate who was down home in Plains, playing softball and meeting with experts. The danger was that our damned-if-you-do, damned-if-you-don't friends in the media would announce that he was overconfident—the Tom Dewey analogy, with Gerald Ford cast as an unlikely Harry Truman. So a compromise was reached for August: He would make a New Hampshire speech the first week, the ABA speech the second week, no speeches the week of the Republican convention (lest we detract from the bloodbath), and a three-speech blitz the week after their convention, to put their candidate on the defensive before he got his act together.

There was talk of Capricorn Records' annual picnic the next week. Its president, Phil Walden, was an early Carter supporter, but his star, Greg Allman, was involved in a messy drug trial. There were suggestions that Carter skip the picnic.

"To me there's more to it than politics," Carter said. "It's friendship. Phil was out raising money for me when nobody else was." He smiled. "Last year Phil wanted me to leave the party before people started drinking too much and taking dope. And when I leave—my staff leaves too!"

Jack Watson outlined the work of his "transition staff." Jack was dark-haired and handsome, brilliant, charming, close to Carter, a law partner of Kirbo's—and while we were out killing ourselves on the campaign he was back in Atlanta calmly making plans for the new administration.

Next, Stu Eizenstat discussed the work of his issues staff. He and Jack presented a dramatic contrast. Both were extremely able lawyers in their thirties, but Jack was the golden boy, and Stu—thin, homely, perpetually worried Stu—was the class grind. A certain rivalry was implicit in their roles, for only one of them could be the top White House domestic adviser, and it was assumed that was the role they both coveted.

Stu spoke of the need to make Soviet violations of the Helsinki human-rights agreements a campaign issue. He argued that human rights was a no-lose issue: Liberals liked to use it against right-wing dictatorships and conservatives saw it as anti-Soviet. Stu's deep concern about Russian discrimination against Jews led directly to Carter's stand on human rights, although others later sought credit for it.

Pat Caddell rattled off some highly favorable poll results. When he said something about "the size of the landslide," Carter broke in: "It's not just ego—tax reform and welfare reform and a lot of other things will depend on our margin of victory."

Pat commented that the Republican candidate, because he would start so far behind, would probably launch a personal attack on Carter.

"That's what I would do," Carter agreed.

Carter spoke of how he did not want to grow isolated, that he wanted his staff to have easy access to him and to give him ideas and criticism. A week later, he was complaining that he never had any privacy because Jody and Greg and I were always hanging around his house.

He mentioned my book *The Presidents' Men*, which I'd given him.

"How many of you have read it?" he asked.

A few hands went up—Jody, Caddell, Rafshoon.

"I want all of you to read it," Carter declared. "It's excellent."

He added, "I was really surprised—I didn't know Pat could write that well."

Ho-ho-ho.

Near the end of the meeting, Carter made a perhaps enigmatic remark: "What I really like is shaking hands in shopping centers and factory shift lines. But I also like sitting at the Pond House for six hours listening to Zbig and Cy Vance and Henry Owen talk about foreign policy. It's two different worlds—but to me it's the same world."

When I repeated that remark to a New York *Times* reporter who was writing a "think piece" on Carter, he shrugged and said all Carter meant was that he could handle different constituencies with equal ease.

I thought Carter was suggesting more, that at best his life had taken on a perfect unity, that there were no loose ends, that everything he did now contributed to the purpose of his life, which was to achieve power and govern wisely. I sometimes thought of him as a man tormented by a dream of perfection, and in those sweet August days the dream must have seemed within his grasp. He could bring together the factory worker and the intellectual, bind up the nation's wounds, and have the greatness he hungered for. He had only to be bold.

Perfection, of course, is more easily dreamed of than achieved, a fact we were reminded of by the next day's misadventures.

Carter had decided to make his support of the American family a major campaign theme. The idea was that various government policies, such as urban renewal, "man in the house" welfare rules, and some tax regula-

tions, harmed the family structure, and he would make sure that all government policies helped, not hurt, families. This was a position that supposedly had great appeal to Catholics and ethnic groups concerned by
signs of moral breakdown in America. His "pro-family" stance would thus
reassure Catholic/ethnic voters who might be worried about his Baptist
religion or his pro-choice position on abortion.

This was all fine, but we had a conflict. Carter had promised Catholic
leaders that his first post-convention speech would be on the family. But
he had also promised his New Hampshire supporters that if he won their
primary he'd return there for his first post-convention speech, which had
been scheduled as a big outdoor rally.

Carter's solution was simplicity itself: He would deliver the pro-family
speech to the New Hampshire audience. Jody and I protested that an
outdoor rally was not the place to address as serious and complex an issue
as family policy. But Carter was determined to do just that. He gave me
four pages of handwritten notes on which he told me to base the speech.
Some of his ideas were very personal:

"The problems of the aged would be reduced if we obeyed the biblical
command to honor our father and mother."

"Some say that income tax exemptions for children encourage large
families. I agree with Senator Mondale: We never discussed tax laws at
that time in my house."

"Have you ever seen an interstate highway go through a golf course?"

"When I was a child, the family was the center of my life. I always knew
where my mama and daddy were—and vice versa."

I wrote a draft, keeping it short so the crowd wouldn't have time to get
bored, and gave it to him on Monday. He said to call later and we'd work
on it, but when I called he said he'd decided to go play softball. He sensed
my dismay; the speech was the next day, and after he approved it, I had to
have it typed and reproduced, not simple matters in our campaign. He
added, almost in apology, "Pat, sometimes I've just *got* to get out of this
house."

I went to his house that night and found him working on the speech.
He wasn't happy.

"This is so bad I hate to release it."

I thought it wasn't a bad speech, and it might have been better if he'd given it priority over softball. Neither of us had anything to add, so I took the speech and left.

The crowd in Manchester the next morning was large and enthusiastic, clearly enjoying the music, the banners, and the bright, cloudless day. As it turned out, they were fascinated by Carter's remarks on the family. People listened intently, because this was something relevant to their lives instead of the usual bombast. The biggest cheers of the day were for Carter's "honor thy father and mother" line.

After the rally, we went to the Wayfarer Inn, where Carter had a private lunch with Joe Califano. The meeting was part of my effort to bring Califano into the campaign, despite the resistance of some of the Georgians. A few days earlier, Carter told me he'd heard that Califano was involved in shady business deals. "Governor," I protested, "he can make so damn much money legally as a Washington lawyer, there's no way he'd do that. If nothing else, he's too smart."

I had an ally in Fritz Mondale. A few days earlier, the three of us had been discussing the family speech and Mondale had urged that Carter put Califano out front as an adviser on family affairs.

"I could call him right now," I said, and when Carter didn't object, I got Califano on the phone and he signed on. He plunged into his new assignment with his customary zeal and soon had task forces grinding out reports, experts gathering statistics, and letters going out to hundreds of Catholic leaders. Joe left no stone unturned where impressing a potential president was concerned.

After lunch with Califano, who made a strong impression on him, Carter proceeded to a reception for local Democrats. It should have been a routine affair. The family speech was our news for the day. But when Carter got up to speak he startled everyone by declaring: "I predict to you that as soon as the Republican convention is held, there is going to be almost an unprecedented vicious personal attack on me."

Zap! There went the family speech. If he'd only said "personal attack" it would have been all right, but "vicious" was a scare word, a newsmaking word on a day when we didn't need more news. I suspected his outburst had been triggered by that day's Manchester *Union-Leader*, which had devoted its front page to warning its readers that the Red devil was arriving from Georgia.

Perhaps sensing his blunder, Carter proceeded to improvise beautifully: "We need to make sure that we can withstand those attacks by one means only. Not by hiding, not by lashing back, but by being immune to successful attacks because we're wrong, or because we're dishonest, or because we lack courage, or because we're divided, or because we're timid. We've got to deserve support. We ought to remember how deeply hurt the American people have been in the last few years. Our basic confidence, our basic trust, our basic faith in our own country has been shaken. I think more than any other time in the last hundred years we feel that something precious has slipped out of our hands. And I feel a tremendous responsibility not to betray the trust of people like you all over the country who have confidence in me. I want to be a little better, a little cleaner, a little more honest, a little harder working, a little closer to you, than I would under ordinary circumstances. Because we are in a time of testing."

Very nice, but wasted. The reporters were already scrambling to get "vicious personal attacks" into their leads. Back on Peanut One, as the media had dubbed our chartered campaign plane, our takeoff was delayed because a TV crew was late.

"The family material really went over well," I told Carter. "But I'm worried that what you said at the reception about vicious attacks may cut into the coverage."

Carter looked at me in astonishment, glanced at his watch, and said he thought it was past the television deadlines for the afternoon.

As it turned out, the family speech was sufficiently original and had been delivered sufficiently early in the day that it was well reported. But the "vicious" line was another example of the candidate's knack for offhand remarks that undercut our positive message. His moments of eloquence didn't make news, but his blunders did, and those of us around him were left with the uneasy feeling that we had a loose cannon on the ship.

6
AND LIKE I WAS . . .

After the New Hampshire trip, I started to work on Carter's August 11 speech to the American Bar Association. He told me he wanted a tough, populist speech, like his Law Day speech, but that wasn't feasible. He'd been a lame-duck governor when he delivered the Law Day speech to the Georgia Bar Association, and the ABA, whatever you thought of it, wasn't the Georgia bar.

He gave me a copy of a handwritten Christmas letter that Julia Coleman, his high school principal, had sent friends in 1960. He attached a note: "Pat: Keep this. Important. Will use in major speech. p 7–8. JC." The passage he'd marked read: "We have to adjust to changing times and still hold out for unchanging principles. It is not easy. But neither education nor religion promises us an easy life. Anyway, I like it better with challenge and effort—with ideals of service to those causes good and true."

It was a nice statement, and I liked the idea of quoting Miss Coleman along with Holmes and Brandeis. We used it in the ABA speech and again in his inaugural address.

I'd finished a first draft when Ann called from Virginia. She was ill and needed me. I flew home and stayed a week, and the speech was finished by Jody and Carter, who had a heated dispute when Carter decided to begin with these lines:

"'We will not lie, cheat or steal, nor tolerate among us those who do.'

"Those words comprise the ancient code of honor which was adopted and is still used by the Air Force and Military Academies."

He went on to argue that the same strict standards should be applied to people in public life.

Jody, who had been expelled from the Air Force Academy for cheating, argued strongly against that opening, but Carter stuck with it. (Jody was generally more nonchalant about the matter; once as we were parked on a runway and an air force jet blasted off, he drawled, "If I'd only learned not to lie and cheat, I'd be flying one of those things.")

Ann was still recovering when I had to return to Georgia, so I took Laura with me, after first calling and getting Rosalynn's assurance that Amy could use a playmate. After we arrived at the Carter home, the two girls ran off to play, and Carter and I discussed the speech he was to deliver in West Virginia the next evening. Then Chip came by and asked my advice on a speech he was giving. Laura and I drove over to Chip and Caron's house trailer and stayed for dinner.

Chip was the middle son and the one who was most interested in politics. He was very much a child of the sixties. He'd smoked dope, avoided Vietnam, and become a Bob Dylan freak, so much so that one winter he and some friends drove nonstop to upstate New York to knock on the singer's door and receive a brief handshake. Carter had met Dylan when Chip invited him to the governor's mansion after a concert in Atlanta one night.

I suggested that Chip might talk in his speech about what kind of father Carter had been. "No," he said firmly, "I never talk about that." Later, Chip expressed annoyance at all the attention that had been paid to his father's smile. Everyone had a smile, he said.

I said I thought his father had a wider range of emotions than most men: He was capable of greater joy, as expressed in his smile, and also of greater anger, as reflected in his equally spectacular scowls. Chip laughed and recalled a picture of his father as governor, leaning across his desk, scowling, with the vein in his temple throbbing. "That's the one I used to see when I brought home report cards that didn't satisfy him."

The next morning Laura and I picked up Amy and brought her back to the Best Western, where they swam while I worked in my room. Then I took the girls to lunch in the motel's dining room. As we were finishing, some tourists recognized Amy and came over with pens and paper placemats for her to sign. I was outraged that anyone would ask an eight-year-old girl for her autograph, but Amy was unperturbed. She scribbled

"Amy" without looking up, and I got us out of there as fast as possible.

I drove to Plains with the girls in the back seat, but when we reached Carter's street it was blocked by a tour bus. I was late to see him, the bus wouldn't budge, and finally I wailed in frustration, "Jee-sus Christ!"

Whereupon a little voice from the back seat squeaked, "*Don't take the Lord's name in vain!*"

Carter was speaking in Charleston, West Virginia, that night before a huge Democratic rally as a favor to Senator Robert Byrd, who was expected to be the next majority leader. I had a chance to talk with Carter and Rosalynn on the drive to the airport in Albany. I mentioned something Caron had told me the night before: that after Ford vetoed the school-lunch bill, free milk for poor children in her class at Plains Elementary School had been cut off. For a while Caron had bought milk for them out of her own pocket, and when she could no longer afford that she spoke to her father and he paid for the milk. I thought it a moving story, one that dramatized the human impact of Ford's vetoes, and I urged Carter to use it that night.

He said he'd enjoyed a piece I'd written for the op-ed page of the New York *Times*, blasting Bill Safire for a nasty column on Carter and his staff.

"It worked out well," I said. "I was surprised he didn't take a shot back at me."

"You didn't leave him much to shoot at," the candidate said admiringly.

We discussed where he should kick off his campaign on Labor Day. He wanted to do it in Georgia, and the choice had come down to Macon or the Warm Springs vacation home where Franklin Roosevelt had died. I argued that Macon meant nothing outside of Georgia, but Warm Springs was a shrine for all Democrats. The drawback was that it was isolated and not well suited for a large crowd. Carter asked his wife what she thought about using Warm Springs. "I like it," she said, and Warm Springs it was.

I brought up Milt Gwirtzman. It was clear to me that, for whatever reason, Carter would not work with Milt, and we needed a new issues person on the plane. Carter agreed entirely. "I've told Stu I don't want him on the plane. I want people around me whose judgment I can trust. If Gwirtzman sends me ten ideas, nine of them aren't any good." (When I repeated that to Greg, he laughed and said, "He ought to see the ones I don't let through to him.")

When we arrived at the auditorium in Charleston that evening, I went to the press room and found Norman Mailer, who was to fly back to Plains with us to interview Carter for the *New York Times Magazine*. The editors had asked me to give him any help I could. I introduced myself and Norman introduced his friend Norris Church, an elegant woman with high cheekbones, red hair, freckles, and a bewitching Arkansas twang.

Norman and I bellied up to the bar, where he opened a can of beer, took a healthy swig, and refilled the can with whiskey. After a while we wandered into the auditorium to hear Carter's speech. He spoke from notes and worked in the story about Caron and the free-milk program.

We'd been deluged with advice on what he should say about the strip mining that had so devastated West Virginia. He was urged by our eco-hawks to call for strong regulation, by Governor Jay Rockefeller's people to fuzz the issue, and by Senator Byrd's people to say nothing. Carter followed Byrd's advice, which led a young man to confront me after the speech.

"How the hell can he come to West Virginia and not talk about strip mining?" he demanded.

I shrugged and walked away. Our campaign left many disillusioned idealists in its wake. The road to the White House, one might say, is paved with disillusioned idealists.

The Charleston airport is notorious for being atop a mountain and often cloaked in fog. When we returned to Peanut One that night you could barely see your hand before your face. Norman Mailer, Norris Church, and I found seats together, and two of us began to drink immoderately. In time we noticed that Peanut One was taxiing around the runway. Not taking off, just taxiing. Someone explained that the pilot thought that if he taxied long enough, our jet engines might burn away the fog.

A few sober souls suggested that perhaps we should spend the night in Charleston, but they were shouted down. Carter of course believed that the Lord wanted him to stay on schedule and he therefore did not fear foggy takeoffs or storm-tossed flights the way other mortals did.

Eventually we got off the ground, and I took Norman forward to meet the candidate. Their first talk centered on the writer's admiration for Carter's ability to Eskimo-roll a kayak, a feat that Norman confessed he had never accomplished. After a while Carter said he was looking forward to their interview the next day, and Norman and I took the hint and returned to our seats.

By the time we landed in Albany, two hours late, I was obsessed with getting to the Best Western, where I'd left Laura with a teenage babysitter. I could have ridden the press bus directly to the motel, but the press bus was notoriously wayward, so I came up with another plan. I would ride in Carter's motorcade to his house in Plains, pick up the rental car I'd left there, and drive to Americus, perhaps beating the press bus by twenty or thirty minutes.

The flaw in my plan was that, while I was quite capable of discussing women, politics, and literature with Norman Mailer, I was in no shape to drive an automobile. I was just outside Plains when a red light started flashing behind me.

I saw it all in an instant:

DRUNKEN SPEECHWRITER SEIZED
"I BARELY KNEW HIM," CARTER SAYS

Instead, I stopped my car and a young trooper politely suggested that the public safety might best be served if he drove me the rest of the way. I accepted his generous offer, and when we arrived at the Best Western—well after the press bus—Laura was safely asleep in our room.

Laura went to church with Amy the next morning (possibly a first in her young life), then off to play, and I met Norman and Norris for a late lunch in Plains, which by then was sprouting fern bars to accommodate all the journalists and tourists. Norman had gone to church with Carter that morning, then interviewed him, and it had not gone well. "I blew it," he kept saying. "I blew it."

It was true. He'd spent most of his hour asking ponderous philosophical questions and had barely given the astonished candidate time to get a word in. I took them on a tour of Plains, to get Norman's mind off his blown interview, and while he poked about I chatted with Norris. She said that a couple of years earlier she'd been teaching school in a little town in Arkansas when Norman came through on a lecture tour, and she'd been with him ever since.

Norman spent the rest of the day in his room at the Best Western preparing for his second interview with Carter. It turned out better. Norman gave up on philosophy and asked simple questions about politics and government, and was rewarded with some excellent answers. There was a nice moment near the end when Mailer remarked that one of his wives had been a Kendrick from Georgia, and Carter declared that his uncle Alton Carter's wife was a Kendrick. Moreover, the candidate and the novelist discovered that they'd both lived in Provincetown around 1950, when Carter was in the navy, whereupon Carter declared, "We may have been there at the same time."

It was an example of Carter's relentless ability to find something in common with everyone. He would meet a woman named Karen and eagerly inform her that he had a daughter-in-law named Caron, or tell an audience of Polish-Americans that Caron hailed from Pulaski County, Georgia—a pronouncement, be it said, that the Poles greeted with thunderous applause. The worst was when he would tell audiences in potato-growing states that their state and Georgia had a lot in common, because the potato and the peanut were the only crops that grew underground.

It was easy to make light of the way Carter gamely sought something in common with everyone he met, yet I also imagined that to be one of his strengths. If there is anything you learn in a national campaign, it is what an incredibly diverse country this is, made up of scores of groups that have nothing in common. Forget the melting pot; we're talking armed camps. If any leader is to unite the country, must he not first know and understand its many factions? If Carter sometimes seemed a chameleon, was he not at least trying to reach out in every possible direction? Whether he was simply reaching for votes, or was driven by a dream of unity, was the question that could not then be answered—that was a matter of faith.

When Norman was leaving the next day, he stopped by the Best Western restaurant, where Laura and I were having lunch. One of the topics we'd discussed on our long, liquid flight back from West Virginia had been our daughters and the ease with which they could twist strong men like ourselves around their little fingers.

Norman bowed to Laura, shook my hand, said, "My congratulations on your daughter," and was gone.

We spent the week of the Republican convention keeping very quiet lest we detract from the Ford-Reagan nutcutting. By then, Greg and Marie's little house in the woods outside Americus had become a haven for us and some of our favorite reporters, including Ed Bradley, Eleanor Randolph,

Jim Wooten, Marty Schram, Curtis Wilkie, and Stan Cloud. It was a place to escape the Best Western, a place to unwind and listen to Emmylou Harris and Fleetwood Mac tapes and laugh at the madness of it all.

Alcohol was by far the drug of choice on the campaign, but there was usually a little marijuana around. One night a couple of reporters and I shared a joint or two at Greg's place. The next morning a third reporter, who'd not been present, joked about our dope-smoking. Concerned, I sought out the person I thought responsible for the leak.

"Hey," I protested, "it could cause me problems if people start talking about dope."

"Cause *you* problems," my friend replied. "If my editor heard I was smoking, he'd take me off the campaign!"

That, in our set, was the ultimate punishment; to be taken off the campaign.

Those were the days when marijuana was being decriminalized in many states, and reformers were predicting legalization in the eighties. Both Carter and Ford endorsed decriminalization, in part because they knew their sons had smoked. Still, it was insane for me to be smoking with reporters. Everyone gossiped, and some tabloid reporter could have blown up a few joints into a great drug scandal. I think we shared those joints for symbolic reasons. The reporters and I were friends, yet the campaign made us adversaries. By smoking, we made a separate peace.

I spent a lot of time with reporters. What I said was off the record and I tried to be candid. They wanted to understand Carter, and I shared my thoughts, but I don't think I often impressed them. I saw complexity where most of them saw only perversity or politics as usual. I thought the man was *interesting*. I remember telling a reporter, "Never underestimate him and never romanticize him." I don't think I ever underestimated him, but I may have romanticized him sometimes. It helped.

I had been fascinated by the state-issued collection of Carter's gubernatorial speeches, which he had given me in early July. In these addresses, he spoke informally, holding little back, trying to communicate, trying to educate, sometimes funny, sometimes passionate, a leader who truly was trying to lead. It I'd been writing about Carter, I'd have thought those speeches a gold mine. I gave the book to reporters for the New York *Times* and the Washington *Post*. Each returned it with a shrug. They would not deign to be impressed by anything as self-serving as speeches. All he was doing was pouring out his soul. They wanted news.

In his acceptance speech in Kansas City in late August, Gerald Ford unveiled a Vision of America that was remarkably like the one Carter had proclaimed at Madison Square Garden, except that it was guaranteed to cost less.

"That's my speech," I raged, as I watched on TV. "Jerry Ford has stolen our vision!"

Indeed, Ford's sudden concern for human rights and the American family was remarkably like Carter's. I had a brief fantasy that I was writing for them both.

The truth is, it was getting crazy in South Georgia. The heat and/or the candidate and/or the demon rum were altering people's minds. We had been through the phase of throwing each other into the Best Western's swimming pool, and now there was a constant threat that someone would throw someone off a balcony or out a window. Sam Donaldson was widely believed to be cracking up. He would be glimpsed, toupee askew, talking to teenage girls, beating on walls with a rubber hose, and muttering incoherently about Jimmy Carter.

(Earlier, some obscure journal had quoted an anonymous Carter aide as calling Sam "the biggest asshole in the world." When Sam saw the quote, he proclaimed, in high dudgeon, "I may be the biggest asshole on this *airplane*. I may be the biggest asshole in *America*. But *surely*, somewhere in the whole wide *world*, there is *someone* who is a bigger asshole than *I* am!")

As the dog days of August stretched on, some of us sought relief in the nightly softball game that was played on a field near Carter's home in Plains. Carter sometimes pitched for the team of strapping Secret Service men who regularly thrashed the News Twisters, an assortment of broken-down reporters who were trying to recapture the glories of yesteryear. After the game, people would adjourn for another drunken night at Faye's Barbecue Villa, a restaurant (loosely speaking) that had been created by parking some house trailers together and filling them with picnic tables and folding chairs. You brought your own booze, and for seven dollars you got a big, overcooked steak and the pleasure of listening to the reporters complain about our candidate and to our people complain about the duplicity of the media. One night we took Norman Mailer and Norris Church there for a taste of the high life. My daughter Laura was with me, and at some point she decided to lie down under the table and go to sleep. But first she tied Norman's shoelaces together—quite normal behavior at Faye's. Those mad nights began to blur together until you feared that you were trapped, like a character in a Beckett play, condemned to stay in Faye's Barbecue Villa, drinking and arguing with those same people, forever.

On Sunday, August 22, we left on a four-day swing that would take us to Los Angeles, to the American Legion convention in Seattle, and—our raid on the Republican heartland—to the Iowa State Fair.

When we arrived in Los Angeles, Carter met with some entertainment-industry executives who wanted to talk about tax shelters. We then proceeded to a reception that Warren Beatty was giving for Carter at the Beverly Wilshire.

A week earlier Maxie Wells, Carter's secretary, had asked Greg and me if there were any movie stars we wanted to meet. "Warren Beatty's giving a reception," she explained, "and they all want to come." I couldn't think of any movie star I wanted to meet, except Liv Ullmann, and I assumed she didn't concern herself with American politics.

Beatty's thirty or forty guests included Faye Dunaway, Robert Altman, Neil Simon, Paul Simon, Diana Ross, Sidney Poitier, Cybill Shepherd, and Hugh Hefner. I introduced myself to Hefner and told him I'd recently met his daughter, Christie, and found her most impressive. (She was twenty-four then and had just gone to work for her father's magazine; when I asked her future goals she smiled sweetly and said, "To run *Playboy*.")

Hefner beamed at the mention of his daughter. "I don't know what the outer limits of paternal pride are," he said, "but I'm about there."

Hefner might have been beaming at more than I imagined. He knew that his magazine would soon publish Bob Scheer's interview with Carter, with its explosive remarks about sex, and that it was certain to cause much controversy and sell many magazines—and did, far more than anyone could have dreamed possible.

I talked to screenwriter Robert Towne. Two years earlier, his *China-*

town had inspired me to write *The President's Mistress* and now my novel's success had led me here to meet him.

I also talked to director Robert Altman, who was very high on something. I greatly admired *Nashville* and *McCabe and Mrs. Miller*, and I asked him which of his movies was his favorite. He insisted it was his then-current bomb, *Buffalo Bill and the Indians*.

I was having a good time, but Carter was not happy to be hobnobbing with movie stars. He considered them frivolous, immoral people and mostly avoided them. I assumed that Pat Caddell, who was friendly with Beatty, had talked him into attending this gathering.

Carter's mood was not improved by Beatty's dumb introduction in which he said that his friends didn't want anything for their support . . . except for him to nationalize the oil companies, free all the political prisoners, and various other far-left causes. Carter made clear, in his opening remarks, that those were not his goals. He added that his presence at Beatty's party should end the criticisms that he was overly moralistic.

When Carter took questions, the celebrities revealed more ego than insight. Carroll O'Connor, TV's Archie Bunker, wanted to know how Carter could criticize a great statesman like Henry Kissinger. James Caan asked if he would visit his son's little league team. Tony Randall asked if Carter would support a federally financed national theater.

A bemused Carter replied that in all his months of campaigning no one had ever asked him that before.

"You've never met with people of this level," Randall said.

"That's why I'm the candidate," Carter said drily.

Jerry Brown wandered in during his remarks, and Carter launched a closing monologue that was both a "more-liberal-than-thou" rebuke to the celebrities and one of the strongest populist statements he would ever make:

"If we make a mistake, the chances are we won't actually go to prison, and if we don't like the public school system, we put our kids in private schools. But the overwhelming majority of the American people are touched directly and personally when government is ill-managed or insensitive or callous or unconcerned about those kinds of problems.

"When the tax structure is modified, which Congress does almost every year, you can rest assured that powerful people who are well organized, who have good lawyers, who have lobbyists in Washington, don't get cheated. But there are millions of people in this country who do get cheated, and they are the very ones who can't afford it.

"We take our transportation for granted. We can go out and get in our Chevrolet or our Buick or our Cadillac or our Rolls Royce and go anywhere we want to. A lot of people don't have automobiles. I can go a mile from my house, I can go two hundred yards from my house, and people are there who are very poor, and when they get sick it's almost impossible for them to get a doctor.

"In the county where I farm, we don't have a doctor, we don't have a dentist, we don't have a pharmacist, we don't have a registered nurse, and people who live there who are very poor have no access to health care. We found in Georgia through a three-year study that poor women, who are mostly black, in rural areas, have twenty times more cervical cancer than white women in urban counties, just because they haven't seen a doctor.

"There's a need for public officials—presidents, governors, congressmen, and others—to bypass the lobbyists and the special-interest groups and our own circle of friends who are very fortunate, and try to understand those who are dependent on government to give them a decent life.

"When people organize, there's an almost built-in separation from the kind of people I've just been describing. Doctors really care about their patients, but when doctors organize and hire a lobbyist, the lobbyist doesn't give a damn about the patients.

"The same with lawyers. . . . The same thing with farmers and with people in business. So I say public servants, like me and Jerry Brown and others, have a special responsibility to bypass the big shots, including you and people like you, and like I was, and to make a concerted effort to understand people who are poor, black, speak a foreign language, who are not well educated, who are inarticulate, who have some monumental problem, and at the same time to run the government in a competent way."

One could not ask for a more eloquent statement on social injustice in America, or of the responsibilities of political leadership. Yet Carter's remarks can't be fully understood apart from their context, the barely disguised rebuke he was delivering to a group of people to whom he felt morally and intellectually superior.

Consider the message between the lines:

". . . we put our kids in private schools." But of course that "we" didn't really include Carter, who often talked about the little integrated public school in Plains that his daughter attended.

"When the tax structure is modified . . . powerful people don't get cheated." Carter, fresh from his meeting with the movie executives, was reminding the movie stars that their industry fought for tax breaks as fiercely as any other special-interest group.

". . . our Cadillac or our Rolls Royce . . ." Carter, of course, owned no Cadillac or Rolls Royce, but he imagined that movie stars did.

"In the county where I farm . . . people are there who are very poor . . . twenty times more cervical cancer . . ." This was one of Carter's more dramatic portrayals of himself as a simple farmer, living among the common folk, doing battle against poverty and injustice and cervical cancer. In fact, to say he "farmed" anywhere was absurd.

"Doctors really care about their patients, but . . . the lobbyist doesn't give a damn about the patients." Carter had it both ways here. Doctors/lawyers/farmers/businessmen all love their patients/clients/customers, but those nasty old lobbyists cause all the trouble. Your could just as well argue that the lobbyists do precisely what their greedy clients want, but that wouldn't let a lot of important people off the hook.

His attack on lobbyists echoed what he'd said two years earlier in his Law Day speech. Indeed, his entire statement was a more focused, angrier version of the Law Day speech. The first had been inspired by his scorn for Ted Kennedy, the second by his scorn for Jerry Brown and the movie-world celebrities.

But he went farther in the second statement.

"So I say public servants, like me and Jerry Brown and others, have a special responsibility to bypass the big shots, including you and people like you, *and like I was . . .*"

Carter thus separated himself from the movie stars and all the big shots who, in his mind, don't care about ordinary people. He declared that he had once been one of them but had somehow changed, had become worthy to govern.

This was no offhand remark. Carter was obsessed with a basic political fact that most of us take for granted, but which he saw as a paradox and an injustice: that even in democracy, a privileged few make decisions for, and control the lives of, a powerless many.

In June of 1971, soon after he became governor, he told a Lions Club convention:

"Instilled within me and within your hearts is an acknowledgment sometimes not spoken. There is a mandatory relationship between the powerful and the influential and the socially prominent and wealthy on the one hand, and the weak, the insecure and the poor on the other.

"This is a relationship not always completely understood. I don't completely understand it myself. But I know that in a free society we do see very clearly that one cannot accept great blessings bestowed on him by God without feeling an inner urge and drive to share those blessings with others of our neighbors who are not quite so fortunate as we."

It was as if his first months as governor had opened his eyes to the sufferings of the poor and the indifference of the rich. His statement was remarkable not only for its eloquence and humility, but for its rather touching assumption that the Lions would feel that "mandatory relationship" and share his "inner urge" to help the poor.

Clearly, Carter's religion made him feel guilty about his wealth, but what was he to do? Give it all away? Reporter Bob Shogan wrote of attending a Sunday school class that Carter taught, after he was president, wherein he told how he was troubled by Christ's admonition to a rich man to give away everything and serve God. Christ was asking more of Carter than he could give, and his failure tormented him. How could he escape the curse of his possessions, of his power?

He never answered the question, in public at least, but in Los Angeles that day, before the movie stars, he nonetheless asserted that he was different, when he spoke scornfully of "the big shots, including you and people like you, *and like I was . . .*"

I think Carter was giving us a glimpse of his private belief that he had been "born again" not only in a religious sense but in a political sense, that he had cast off the sin of privilege and become one with the people he wished to serve. I think he had come to see his campaign, his long and punishing march to the presidency, as a rite of purification, an ordeal that purged him and made him worthy to govern.

He must have seen—even an outsider can see—echoes of biblical epic in his life. There is Carter as the prodigal son, returning home from distant lands (his naval career) to comfort his dying father, to search his soul, and finally to take up his father's responsibilities. There are parallels between the South, defeated, disgraced, cut off from national leadership, and the Jewish people, exiled and dispossessed. There is Carter in his early political career, challenging the lobbyists and lawyers, forever seeking to drive the moneychangers from the temple of government. There is Carter suffering political defeat in 1966, looking into his soul and finding the sin of pride, being "born again," and thereafter running like a man possessed, never breaking stride until he reached the White House.

There is Carter, mocked by the "big shots" early in his presidential campaign, but drawing strength from his small circle of disciples, traveling about, sleeping on friends' sofas, washing (if not their feet) his own socks each night, proving his humility and worthiness to lead. There are so many other touches: Carter the carpenter, the black murderess brought in to care for his daughter, the visits to outcasts in prisons and mental institutions, the endless effort to do God's work on earth. He injected religious terms into his speeches: his supporters were making a "sacrificial" effort, our system of government is still "immaculate."

Did Carter, to put it crudely, have a Jesus complex? Did he, in one corner of his heart, see himself as a savior, whose mission it was to heal a sinful land? He would deny it ("I don't look on the presidency with religious connotations," he told Bill Moyers), but there would be more evidence of it in the days ahead, and those who seek to understand the man would do well to look in that direction.

We'd had several days to prepare for Carter's August 23 speech to the Town Hall Forum in Los Angeles. The audience would be important civic leaders, the speech would be carried on statewide radio, and we wanted a major address. At the outset, I talked with Stu, who urged that the speech be more reflective than political, to contrast Carter's seriousness with the chaos of the recent Republican convention. Just what Carter should reflect on was left to me.

My instinct, as it had been when I joined the campaign three months earlier, was to state a rationale for Carter's presidency, to explain that it would not be a fluke, as many people still seemed to think, but that it in fact possessed a historical inevitability. I began by again detailing the "national nightmare" of war, assassinations, scandals, and political disillusion that had afflicted America since 1963. "Small wonder, then, that the politics of 1976 have turned out to be significantly different from years past. I doubt that four years ago or eight years ago a former southern governor with no national reputation and no Washington experience would have been able to win the Democratic nomination for president. But this year many voters were looking for new leaders, leaders who were not associated with the mistakes of the past."

I proceeded to some new thoughts on why Carter would be president, ideas I'd been mulling over since I had observed Jody and Hamilton alongside the two Mondale men at Hilton Head and had reflected on how much tougher and hungrier the two Georgians were.

"As I have observed the political world in recent years, it has seemed to me that there is a process at work, in both political parties and probably in all nations, by which over a period of time the political leadership becomes isolated from, and different from, the people they are supposed to serve.

"It seems almost inevitable that if political leaders stay in power too long, and ride in limousines too long, and eat expensive meals in private clubs too long, they are going to become cut off from the lives and concerns of ordinary Americans. It is almost like a law of nature—as Lord Acton said, power tends to corrupt.

"I think this process reached a peak a few years ago, when we had a president who surrounded himself with people who knew everything in the world about merchandising and manipulation and winning elections, and nothing at all about the hopes and fears and dreams of average people.

"When government becomes cut off from its people, when its leaders are talking only to themselves instead of addressing reality, then it is time for a process of national self-renewal, time to look outside the existing governing class for new leaders with new ideas. I think that is what happened in the Democratic party this year. I think our party was ready for renewal, for new faces, for a changing of the guard. If the candidate had not been myself, I think we would have chosen someone else who was not part of the old order of things."

The next section of the speech was more political. Our issues staff had prepared an analysis of Ford's fifty-odd vetoes, and I blasted the vetoes and declared that Ford's policies hit hardest "on those people who are weakest, who are poor and uneducated and isolated, who are confused and inarticulate, who are often unemployed and chronically dependent—in short, those members of society whom a good government would be trying hardest to help."

Carter, Jody, Greg, and I discussed the speech in Carter's study on Sunday morning, before we left for Los Angeles. Carter had added various words and phrases but left the thrust of the speech intact. Mostly we debated minor points. Carter had changed "my home in Plains" to "my farm in Plains," but Jody persuaded him he was only inviting ridicule if he kept calling himself a farmer. We cut specific references to Nixon, mostly because we found the use of his name distasteful. My section on the vetoes asked: "Doesn't it make more sense to spend money on milk and education today, to help children get a fair start in life, than to spend money on police and courts and jails ten years from now?" Stu had objected that this was the kind of liberal cause-and-effect that couldn't be proved, but Carter liked the line and it stayed.

In his stump speeches, Carter sometimes mentioned the rising gonorrhea rate among children. I liked that touch of realism and put it in this speech. He went me one better, adding teenage suicide, so the passage concluded: "I sensed that some people thought I shouldn't use those words, suicide and gonorrhea, because they are ugly words describing unpleasant facts. But there are many unpleasant problems in our society—children who need food, overcrowded jails and mental institutions, inadequate treatment for the young men who were maimed in Vietnam, and the heartbreak and family disintegration that unemployment can bring.

"All these are ugly problems, and it is a natural human instinct for us to want to tune them out. But we cannot tune them out. We can only succeed in tuning out our own humanity, including those qualities of compassion and concern without which no society, however rich or powerful, can be truly great."

We went over the speech line by line until Carter was satisfied. He overruled a number of Greg's suggestions, and when he finally used one he commented, "We have to throw Greg a crumb now and then." But in general Carter was at his best in these sessions: open-minded, wry, and more often right than wrong. My impression was that he enjoyed the intellectual challenge of editing speeches far more than he enjoyed delivering them. Whatever my other complaints about Carter, it was almost always a pleasure to focus on a speech with him. We both cared about words—about their sounds and silences and ambiguities, about their potential to shame and delight and inspire—and he had, I thought, developed a certain grudging respect for my talents.

The Town Hall Forum speech went well. We issued advance copies, the reporters were impressed, the audience was enthusiastic, and Carter's delivery was excellent. Jim Wooten wrote in the New York *Times* that the speech "was smoothly constructed and seemed to match the rhythms and patterns of his southern speech." (If the latter was true, it was through no conscious effort on my part; I just wrote simple English and hoped for the best.) There was one flap: Carter had been driven around Los Angeles in a Secret Service limousine, a fact reporters quickly pounced on, so we dropped the reference to politicians who rode around in limousines.

Coverage of the speech was very good, although inevitably it focused more than I liked on the attack on Ford's vetoes and less than I'd hoped on the reflective passages. We eventually stopped criticizing Ford's vetoes because, however much they might outrage liberals, the average voter thought they saved him money.

Carter had written "Good job!" on my original draft of the speech, and the day after its delivery, when I sent him a memo on the media reaction, he wrote in the margin: "Pat—you did a fine job on this— J." Two compliments on one speech! It never happened again.

For me, Stu's objection to my line about spending money on schools today instead of jails tomorrow and Carter's decision to use it nonetheless pretty well sum up the dynamic of the 1976 campaign. There was nothing unusual about Stu's advice. It was what the overwhelming majority of Democratic political consultants and campaign aides would have said, then and now. Cool down the rhetoric, play it safe. It was Carter's peculiar genius to be willing to make that leap of faith on schools and jails, and elsewhere to speak without embarrassment of love and compassion, both because his religious impulse told him it was right and because his political instinct told him it would work, that after the venality of Nixon, America was ready for his brand of idealism.

The acceptance speech, the remarks at Warren Beatty's reception, and the Town Hall Forum speech marked the liberal, or perhaps populist, peaks of the campaign. Carter was far ahead in the polls, supremely confident, and willing to speak out boldly. If, in later years, any Democratic nominee for president spoke so passionately about social injustice in America, I am unaware of it. The coming of Reaganism shifted the political dialogue sharply to the right. Terrible social problems were ignored as many Democrats joined Republicans in deploring crime, denouncing taxes, and wooing blue-collar voters and the middle class. Carter's best speeches in 1976 reflected not only his religion and basic decency, but also the lingering idealism of the Roosevelt-Truman and Kennedy-Johnson eras, the belief that America had the heart and the means to solve its social problems. Once Reagan slashed taxes on the rich and ran the national debt to unimagined levels, it became difficult for any informed person to argue that those problems could be solved. The Gipper had given away the store.

The first time Carter and I discussed his speech to the American Legion, I asked how he wanted to handle the amnesty issue. "I want to meet it head-on," he said, and he did. He stood before a huge gathering of Legionnaires in Seattle and, near the end of a serious and well-received speech, restated his well-known promise to issue a pardon for draft evaders. The audience responded with about forty-five seconds (it seemed an eternity) of booing and cries of "No, no!" That was pretty much it for the American Legion speech. We rationalized that a lot of people would admire Carter for speaking his mind. Still, it was hard to argue that having your candidate booed on the evening news was a big plus.

The Iowa State Fair the next day was a festive occasion and Carter was in high spirits. He departed from his text often, including one quite fascinating digression on the art of growing peanuts. It was a fine speech, but soon a flap arose, the inevitable flap. In the speech, Carter had promised to end the food embargos that farmers so bitterly resented. But in a news conference he had conceded that there could be emergencies in which he would resort to an embargo. So the story became "Carter Flip-flops," and our four-day swing ended on a sour note.

August had brought unexpected problems. The New Hampshire speech was marred by Carter's "vicious personal attacks" remark. He reluctantly met with Ralph Nader, although he thought it hurt him with small businessmen who hated Nader. He was photographed with Warren Beatty and thought that did him no good. The American Legion speech ended in boos and the Iowa State Fair speech with flip-flop stories. On the last day of the month he met with some Catholic bishops, who proceeded to sandbag him by telling reporters they were disappointed with his stand on abortion.

Meanwhile, Jerry Ford had gotten himself nominated, was back in the White House trying to look presidential, and was creeping up in the polls.

That was the situation when Carter, Mondale, and their senior staffs met at the Pond House in early September. Carter was in good spirits. His attitude was that there'd been a few minor problems, but it would all be fine once he got back to the people.

"Just get me back to the shopping centers and the factory shift lines," he kept saying. He pressed Hamilton hard on that: no more big shots and fat cats, no more platforms filled with politicians, just a campaign that went straight to the people.

Fritz Mondale had a request, too. He'd been out campaigning, he said, and it was going well, but there was one thing bothering him. He wasn't sure he understood the *themes* of this campaign, and he wondered if someone could put them on paper.

Poor Fritz Mondale. He was a good soldier, with an orderly, conventional mind, and he wanted to play by the book—if someone would *show* him the damn book. Carter obligingly instructed me to draw up a statement of the themes of the Carter-Mondale campaign. I wrote a little essay and sent it to Carter, but it was wasted effort. His campaign defied neat explanation, for it was rooted in his complexities. Ultimately, the theme was Carter, whatever you chose to see in him. It could be as simple as his smile or as complex as the endless enigma those of us close to him glimpsed. For better or worse, Carter was the campaign.

7
LUST

It was in September that *Playboy* published our candidate's confession that he lusted for women other than his wife, but lust had been a popular feature of the campaign long before that. Our little drama was being played out in that brief, golden era after the dawn of the sexual revolution and before the sudden darkness of AIDS. We on the staff, and our traveling companions in the media, were mostly young, and some of us were open to romantic adventure, or at least to brief escapes from the dehumanizing pressures of politics. In the here-today-gone-tomorrow world of the campaign, the distance from "Hey, it's great to meet you!" to "Let's go up to my room" was often measured in minutes. We raced about America in a state of abandon that was new, exciting, and—for those unaccustomed to such freedom—often scary as hell.

In late August I went home for the first time in two weeks, and Ann and I slipped away for a weekend at the Homestead. I knew I wouldn't be able to get back to Virginia after Labor Day, and out on one of the hiking trails I had an idea.

"Why don't you come to Atlanta for the rest of the campaign?" I suggested. "You can work in the headquarters and write this damn women's speech that's coming up. I'll be gone all week, but on weekends I'll come to Atlanta or you can drive to Americus."

"OK," said Ann, who was as unflappable as she was beautiful, and soon she drove her little Datsun down to Atlanta with one-year-old Michael in the backseat. Thus did the speechwriter preserve his sanity and, for a time, his marriage.

Carter officially began his campaign on Labor Day at Roosevelt's vacation home in Warm Springs. Our caravan left the Best Western before dawn, and as we neared the Roosevelt property, now a national park, we passed thousands of people streaming in on foot. Some squeezed into the small space outside the vacation home, and many more listened over loudspeakers from farther back amid the pines. It was a cool, bright, festive morning. Graham Jackson, the old musician who'd been immortalized by a photo of him tearfully playing his accordion as FDR's funeral train passed by, was there playing "Anchors Aweigh" and "Happy Days Are Here Again." (Someone later told me of the hard negotiations that preceded his appearance; nostalgia can be expensive.)

Carter rewarded the cheering crowd with a spirited address based on a draft of mine that he considerably improved. He opened with a tribute to Roosevelt, and compared Gerald Ford with FDR's opponent in 1932, Herbert Hoover. He also used a Harry Truman quote about the Republicans being the party of the rich and privileged and ours the party of the people. But his biggest applause line was pure Carter, and he shouted it out: "When there's a choice between welfare and work, let's go to work!"

The theme of the speech was leadership, a point he made most memorably in another passage of pure Carter:

"When Harry Truman was in the White House a sign on his desk said, 'The buck stops here.' There was never any doubt who was captain of the ship.

"Now no one seems to be in charge.

"Every time another ship runs aground—CIA, FBI, unemployment, deficits, welfare, inflation, Medicaid—the captain hides in his stateroom while the crew argues about who is to blame."

His original version had been even more vivid, with the buck "running all over Washington" and Captain Ford jumping overboard. We persuaded him those metaphors might be a bit too vivid.

My favorite line was this:

"As a political candidate, I owe the special interests nothing. I owe the people everything."

He said that many times and it always moved me, because I believed it was true, and was the great hope of his presidency.

From the highlight of Warm Springs, it took the campaign only thirty-six hours to reach its absolute low; our arrival the next evening in Scranton, Pennsylvania. As we pulled into the Hilton Inn at nine-thirty, the motorcade was surrounded by a howling mob of anti-abortion demonstrators. I could see Carter getting out of his car and the crowd pushing and shoving his Secret Service men. We fought our way into the hotel, only to find that the room reservations were screwed up and the elevators didn't work. Outside, the right-to-lifers had regrouped across the street to sing "God Bless America" all night. Thus inspired, I did a final rewrite of the next day's human-rights speech.

This speech climaxed Stu Eizenstat's long battle to put human rights at the forefront of the campaign. Initially, I think, Carter didn't share Stu's deep emotional concern for the rights of Russian Jews (few people did), nor was it his instinct to identify with political prisoners around the world. But Carter was drawn to the issue because it put him on high moral ground and because it promised to win him friends among Jewish leaders who were skeptical about him.

Two professors had submitted drafts of a human-rights speech, both hopelessly dull. Then Richard Holbrooke, of our issues staff, wrote a good draft. I summoned him to the plane and we rewrote the speech together, and went over it several times with Carter. He toned it down a little—he cut one reference to political repression in Iran, for example, lest it "tie my hands" in dealings with the Shah—but this remained a strong speech that demanded an end to the cynicism of the Nixon-Kissinger foreign policy and called for the use of American might on behalf of freedom around the world.

By some miracle, which I attributed to Stu, the speech was delivered at a time and place—early afternoon, to a B'nai B'rith convention in Washington, D.C.—where it received maximum media attention. It was a serious speech, one that gave meaning to Carter's generalities about "a government as good as its people," and it got the campaign off to an excellent start.

I spent the rest of the day writing a memo to Carter about our problem with the issues staff. My memo arose from talks with Dick Holbrooke. Dick, later an assistant secretary of state, had been a joy to work with on the human-rights speech. He stressed that our issues people in Atlanta thought they had ideas and material that could help the candidate, but somehow they never seemed to get used. I saw the same problem from the plane. We desperately needed fresh ideas that Carter could use to make news, but we never seemed to have any, or any that he liked, in usable form.

In part this was an organizational problem. I've been in Mexican whorehouses that were better organized than the Carter campaign. But part of the problem was that Carter was ambivalent about "issues." Once I told him I'd try to get him a new idea from Atlanta every day, and he responded with enthusiasm. But as the campaign continued he grew more and more suspicious of new ideas, issues that might somehow back-fire, and more inclined to return to the "themes"—honesty, compassion, trust—that had served him so well.

His senior advisers were also anti-issues. The day after the human-rights speech I commented to Hamilton on how well it had gone, and he replied, "I wouldn't care if Jimmy never made another speech like that. I just want him to hit our basic themes, over and over." Another time, Jerry Rafshoon told me Carter must keep hitting the themes, and nothing else, because then the media would be forced to report them. In truth, if we didn't give the reporters substance, they simply found negative stories to report.

The fact was that almost every time Carter delivered a solid speech on a major issue, as he had on foreign policy and human rights, he received good coverage. We just weren't doing it often enough. Carter might de-liver one news-making speech a week, but then we'd get clobbered on the evening news the other six nights.

Part of the problem was that Milt Gwirtzman was still the issues man on the plane, despite Carter's having told me weeks before that he wanted him replaced. When I later asked Carter about this, he said he'd talked to Stu, but Stu had stressed how Milt had worked so many months with-out pay and we owed it to him to keep him on. I couldn't believe it. The presidency is hanging in the balance, and we're worried about hurting the feelings of one Washington lawyer?

The problem had been made even worse—something I would not have thought possible—when Stu sent a second issues man on the plane, a big, loud, abrasive, self-serving Washington lawyer whom Carter soon ignored.

The situation was maddening. The Atlanta issues staff, according to

Holbrooke, was in despair because they saw these two outsiders standing between them and the candidate. There was a feeling that Stu, whom everyone liked and admired, was overimpressed with these two because they were Washington lawyers. Our issues people were also angry because Stu had brought in Ted Sorensen, Ted Van Dyk, and other Kennedy and Humphrey people to head up planning for the Carter-Ford debates.

Everyone would have been happy if Stu had been willing to join us on the plane, but he wasn't. He felt he should be in Atlanta overseeing his staff, and he didn't want to leave his family and lead our nomadic life.

In my memo to Carter I argued that we should rid ourselves of the various Kennedy "retreads" and make more use of Holbrooke and others on our issues staff who knew his positions and whose loyalty to him was unquestioned. I was not perfectly objective, given my annoyance at the Kennedy crowd during the national convention, but Holbrooke had convinced me there was a larger issue involved. I wrote with trepidation; my job was to produce speeches, not to reorganize the campaign. But with the presidency at stake, I felt that Carter deserved my unvarnished opinions.

I gave Greg the memo to pass along to Carter. Later in the day, he returned it to me with a note: "Pat. I strongly recommend not giving this to Jimmy. I will, of course, if you want me to. I've experienced his reaction to staff criticisms on a few occasions and it is not pleasant. Jody concurs. I suggest you talk to him. GS."

Greg's advice left me frustrated and uncertain. I didn't doubt his sincerity; he thought he was sparing me the candidate's wrath. I didn't bother to talk to Jody, because I assumed he thought I'd overstepped myself. The underlying reality was that as long as there was no strong issues voice on the plane, Jody retained that role by default.

I agonized for a while and finally decided that if the two people closest to Carter didn't think he wanted my advice, then to hell with it. It was a failure of nerve, the one thing I did on the campaign that I regret.

I flew back to Atlanta to help Ann get settled. With the addition of Ann, who was helping both me and Mary Hoyt, my little speechwriting staff now numbered four. I'd hired Bill Keel, a gruff, bald, talented newspaperman with whom I'd worked in Nashville and who had later been the top aide to a powerful Tennessee congressman. I used Bill as my eyes and ears in Atlanta, keeping in touch with the issues staff, the political staff, and the schedulers.

Most important, in late July we'd hired Jim Fallows to back me up. Jim, still in his twenties, was tall and thin—he'd avoided Vietnam by starving himself down below the army's minimum weight limit—and deceptively mild-mannered. A native of California, he was a Harvard graduate and Rhodes scholar who'd worked for Ralph Nader and begun making a name as a magazine writer.

A presidential candidate delivers two basic types of speeches: substantive and rhetorical. In the former, he goes before various interest groups—made up of Jews, teachers, farmers, whomever—and demonstrates his mastery of their issues and that those issues are dear to his heart. The rhetorical speeches, delivered mostly to party rallies, are intended to stir the passions of the faithful.

To me, the substantive speeches were a chore and the rhetorical speeches a joy. Rhetoric—vision—was in my mind what a presidential campaign was all about. The right kind of rhetoric can inspire and unite the nation; the wrong kind uses hate and fear to divide it. As the fall progressed, I concentrated on the political speeches and assigned as many of the policy speeches as possible to Jim, who handled some real monsters—crime, defense, farm policy—with great skill. My assignments in part reflected the fact that my approach to politics was more visceral and Jim's more intellectual. Beyond that, only a fool would write a speech on farm policy if he had someone else to do it.

Jim and I could keep up with the speeches that had to be written, but in time I began to fear that Carter needed someone with more political experience who could give him the tough attack lines that would get him on the evening news. I'd had a call from Bill Haddad, who'd been a political operative for the Kennedys and who wanted to help us if he could. I began to think he might be the politically astute writer we needed. I was aware that if Haddad got on the plane he might render me obsolete, but I decided that for Carter to win was more important than my status—a decision probably unprecedented in presidential politics. Jim was in Plains, working with Carter on a speech, and I asked him to tell Carter that I suggested we hire Haddad. Jim reported back that Carter had been outraged at the idea of spending money on a third speechwriter.

Ann and one-year-old Michael had moved into a little apartment her mother owned in Buckhead. Ann would drop our son off at the Garden of

Eden Day Care Center each morning, spend the day at Carter headquarters, then pick him up and return to the apartment. One night I arrived to find Ann with Michael in her arms, singing "Sweet Kentucky Babe" as he dropped off to sleep. It was for me the most beautiful moment of the autumn, just as the scene a few days before, after the human-rights speech, when I pulled away from a Washington hotel with Laura crying on the sidewalk, was the most terrible. Those three were my real life; the campaign was a fantasy, a siren's song, that kept calling me back.

On Tuesday, September 14, I was about to have dinner at a motel in Sioux Falls, South Dakota, when a reporter asked if I knew that President Ford was going to deliver his official campaign kickoff speech the next day at the University of Michigan. I didn't know that, of course. Why would anyone bother to tell me that? The reporter added that, since Carter was speaking the same evening to an AFL-CIO convention in nearby Dearborn, reporters would certainly compare the two speeches and perhaps bill them as a kind of debate.

I agreed. The question was what we could come up with on short notice. I remembered Jim Fallows mentioning that Jerry Jazinowski, an elegant and astute economist on our issues staff, had sent us a nine-point analysis of Nixon-Ford economic failures. At the time I'd said, "Oh hell, Jim, nine of anything is too many," but now I read Jazinowski's paper, saw that it was solid material, and asked Jim to convert it into a speech.

Jim gave me his draft late that night, and I awoke at dawn thinking it needed more rhetoric. Not wanting to wake Jim—we were sharing a room—I went into the bathroom and wrote a new beginning that hailed the tradition of the Democratic Party, then closed with the repeated use of the phrase "Once the people rule again . . ."

That night Carter delivered our hurriedly assembled speech. Our indictment of Nixon-Ford policies gave reporters something solid to chew on, and many papers carried all nine points. Once again, when we gave the media something substantive, it paid off.

Although our economic critique made the news, I liked my rhetoric better. Except in his acceptance speech, Carter had said little about the Democratic Party's tradition, both because he was running as an outsider and because he wasn't by nature much of a party man. I felt strongly that

the two parties embodied distinct political philosophies and it was important to draw the line. If we couldn't do that before an AFL-CIO convention in Michigan, where could we? Thus, Carter said in part:

"I understand that my opponent made his kickoff speech today in
Michigan, and some people say that tonight marks the official start of the
campaign of 1976.

"I'm glad to see his final and reluctant emergence from the Rose Garden, but I think in a larger sense this presidential campaign began a long
time ago. My opponent and I and the two parties we represent do not exist
in isolation. We are part of the currents of history.

"In that sense this campaign was under way in 1932, when his party
nominated Herbert Hoover and ours nominated Franklin Roosevelt. . . .

"Roosevelt proposed a twenty-five-cent-an-hour minimum wage.
Twenty-five cents. The Democratic Congress finally passed it, but 95 percent of the Republicans in Congress voted against it.

"He gave Rural Electrification to farm homes like mine. He thought
people ought to have security in their old age and he put forward Social
Security. There were ninety-five Republican House members, and ninety-
four voted against Social Security. . . .

"This campaign has been joined a hundred times over, whenever our
party has fought for legislation that would benefit the average American—for Social Security, for minimum wage laws, for Rural Electrification, for voting rights, for civil rights, for Medicare—and our opponent's
party has fought against all that progress."

Perhaps we were preaching to the choir, but it was good to remind the
unionists—it was good to remind the candidate—that this party of ours,
for all its faults and failures, has known greatness.

The AFL-CIO speech, which Jim and I literally produced overnight,
reflected one of the strengths of our campaign: We could turn on a dime.
In one sense, any candidate running against an incumbent president is
hopelessly outmatched. The opposition has Air Force One, state-of-the-
art communications, and unlimited backup staff. I, by contrast, spent the
campaign begging secretaries to type our candidate's speeches. Yet I
thought we had the advantage. I imagined my counterpart in the Ford
campaign surrounded by committees and political consultants. In a pinch,
I could produce a speech in an hour. Jody might glance at it if he had time;

Greg might urge a cut or two, but that was the extent of our bureaucracy. We were the guys in a PT boat, running circles around the White House dreadnought.

A digression on the candidate's humor

Carter told a joke to the AFL-CIO audience, and he was not telling many jokes those days. He'd used the "Little Veteran" joke twice that I knew of, to the union group in May and the American Legion in August; he apparently viewed it as red meat to toss to unruly trade-unionists and old soldiers. In Dearborn he told his "fifty-dollar" joke, which was an example of what I called his Sunday-school humor: the kind of naughty-but-nice joke that preachers tell to prove they're regular fellows.

Briefly, the fifty-dollar joke concerned a shy young divinity student "who was very proud of his personal purity." While eating alone in a crowded restaurant, he was joined by a beautiful young woman. He explained that he was a divinity student and didn't go out with girls. Suddenly she said, very loudly, "*Come up to your room?*"

People at nearby tables laughed, the divinity student stammered his protests, and the young woman added, "*And spend the night?*" He pleaded with her to stop tormenting him, and the young woman smiled and explained that she was a psychology student who'd been assigned to embarrass a shy person in a public place.

Whereupon the divinity student said, very loudly, "FIFTY DOLLARS?"

Later in the campaign Carter told the story about the country storekeeper who liked to quote a Bible verse each time he rang up a sale. One day, during a rain, a city slicker entered his store. The city slicker was driving a Cadillac and pulling a horse trailer, and he needed a blanket to keep his horse dry. The storekeeper said he had one for two dollars. "Look, I've got a million-dollar horse out there," the city slicker said. "Haven't you got a better blanket than that?" Eventually, the storekeeper satisfied the city slicker by selling him the two-dollar blanket for one hundred dollars. As he rang up the sale, he quoted, "He was a stranger, and we took him in."

Do we detect a common thread running through these jokes? (Dare I call them parables?) In each case, the protagonist—the defiant Little Veteran, the shy divinity student, the canny old storekeeper—is a Little Fellow, putting in their places the big bullies, uppity women, and city slickers of the world. That of course is how Carter presented himself, and perhaps saw himself, as a mild-mannered but spunky little fellow, picked on sometimes, but always getting the best of the big bullies because he was canny and honest and pure. George Wallace had played the Little Fellow, too, but his was a nasty little man. Carter's alter ego was out of Horatio Alger, with a touch of Frank Capra thrown in, a Sunday-school hero writ large.

Carter's Sunday-school jokes had little to do with his very caustic private humor. For example, Doris Kearns came to interview him that summer. It was well known that in her book on Lyndon Johnson, Kearns had said that he would sit by her bed at the LBJ Ranch, but that the relationship had not been sexual. Kearns came to Plains soon after having a baby and was understandably drawn. After meeting her, Carter commented, "Now that I've seen her, I understand why Johnson didn't get in bed with her."

Carter's speech to the AFL-CIO had battled Ford's kickoff speech to a draw. Two nights later, in Hot Springs, Arkansas, he used some remarks I'd written about Ford's speech:

"The other night my opponent reluctantly emerged from the Rose Garden and finally made his first speech of the campaign. He spoke of his vision of America. And it was a fine vision, a noble vision. The only trouble was that my opponent has spent his entire life in politics opposing the programs that might make that vision come true.

"He seems to have experienced a remarkable conversion at this late date in his political life.

"But I don't think the people will be fooled. Mr. Ford cannot rhapsodize about the future as if he and his party had no past. The Republican Party from Hoover and McKinley to Coolidge and Nixon has been the party of negativism and opposition." And so on.

Carter opened that speech with some funny lines of his own about Secretary of Agriculture Earl Butz, a man he seemed genuinely to loathe. He began by saying that Butz "predicted that when I was elected president he would be fired. That's the first accurate prediction that Earl Butz has made in a long time."

"I made a speech last spring to the Gridiron Club in Washington, and my good friend Earl Butz was there, and he walked up to me and said, 'Governor, I understand that everywhere you go, you promise that you are going to fire me if you are elected.' I said, 'Yes sir, that's right.' 'But why do you have to say it more than once?' I said, 'First of all, it's my best applause line. Also, in a lot of places the farmers are very discouraged and it gives them something to look forward to next year.'"

On Sunday, September 19, we flew to St. Louis for a dinner honoring Harry Truman. In delivering his speech, Carter piously changed a Truman quote about doing his damndest to doing his darndest. That seemed ironic the next day, when the *Playboy* interview broke, and his remarks about "lust" and "shacking up" inflamed the nation; at that point, whether or not he'd said Truman did his damndest seemed like tame stuff indeed.

On Monday morning we left Manhattan's Penn Station for a whistlestop train ride across New Jersey and Pennsylvania that was supposed to invoke memories of Truman's 1948 journey. Carter had insisted on making "the family" the day's theme. I thought this was crazy—the story would be the journey itself—and after a few halfhearted "family" speeches from the back of the train he reverted to his stump speech. Joe Califano was brokenhearted; he'd produced a thick study, entitled "Report on the American Family," which we gave to reporters and they quickly forgot.

While Carter popped out every hour or so to speak from the back of the train, the rest of us played poker and told stories. In the late afternoon, Charlie Mohr of the New York *Times*, the toughest and best-informed reporter covering the campaign (and, indeed, one of the great reporters of his generation), came running down the aisle with a Xerox copy of the juicy parts of Carter's *Playboy* interview. Charlie was beside himself; he was like a little boy with a dirty book.

I glanced over Carter's remarks about lust and shacking up and shrugged them off. It struck me as a candid and revealing interview. And it was. But it was also political dynamite, which Charlie saw and I did not.

The dimensions of the disaster were not immediately clear. Reporters asked Carter about the interview but he brushed their questions aside.

That evening, several of us were playing poker in Carter's car at the back of the train. We'd keep on playing when the train would pull into a station and Carter would go out to speak. At one stop, after night had fallen, we heard him saying "Bye, y'all, bye y'all" to the crowd as the train left the station. Then we were out of town, gathering speed, and he kept saying "Bye, y'all" into the darkness, into the empty night. Perhaps he had begun to sense what lay ahead.

Bob Scheer had traveled extensively with us that spring while he worked on his *Playboy* interview. Bob was bearded, bright, and sardonic, and enjoyed matching wits with Carter's staff. His previous assignment had been a *Playboy* interview with our rival Jerry Brown. Once I pressed Scheer on the rumors that Brown was gay.

"Come on," I said, "don't you think he might have tried it once, out of intellectual curiosity?"

"No, you don't understand," Scheer insisted. "He'd have tried *heterosexual* sex once, out of intellectual curiosity."

I enjoyed Scheer's company but Carter did not. Scheer was a political radical and a relentless interviewer whose specialty was to ask the most obnoxious questions possible, hoping to goad his subject into self-revelation—Scheer torture, his editor at *Playboy* called it. In Carter's case, this took the form of endless questions about his religion and whether it would make him a puritan president, somehow intolerant of gays, atheists, or other nonconformists. Vainly did Carter protest that he didn't care what people did in the bedroom.

Aside from both possessing world-class egos, Scheer and Carter were about as dissimilar as two intelligent American men could be. The basic problem was that each of them—the Berkeley radical and the Southern Baptist moderate—considered the other a freak. Not surprisingly, the long series of interviews with Scheer was driving Carter up the wall. His final outburst, delivered on his front porch as Scheer was finally leaving for good, contained his controversial remarks on sex, and can best be understood as a rebuke to Scheer and an attempt to have the last word.

Carter began by talking about how much his religion meant to him.

Abruptly, he made a leap: "What Christ taught about most was pride, that one person should never think he was any better than anybody else." (I would have said what Christ taught most about was love, but no matter.) Carter related Christ's parable about the Pharisee who thanked the Lord for making him better than other people, as contrasted with the man who threw himself on the floor and said, "Lord, have mercy on me, a sinner."

I have no doubt that in Carter's mind, Scheer was the arrogant Pharisee, and he was the humble sinner. It was a parable that Carter must often have pondered, as he fought an endless inner battle between his acute sense of superiority and the humility that his religion demanded.

Carter went on to say: "I try not to commit a deliberate sin. I recognize that I'm going to do it anyhow, because I'm human and I'm tempted. And Christ set some almost impossible standards for us. Christ said, 'I tell you that anyone who looks on a woman with lust has in his heart already committed adultery.'

"I've looked on a lot of women with lust. I've committed adultery in my heart many times. This is something that God recognizes I will do—and I have done it—and God forgives me for it. But that doesn't mean that I condemn someone who not only looks on a woman with lust but who leaves his wife and shacks up with somebody out of wedlock.

"Christ says, 'Don't consider yourself better than someone else because one guy screws a whole bunch of women while the other guy is loyal to his wife.'"

What is the point of this sermon? On the face of it, Carter is telling Scheer what a tolerant, open-minded fellow he is. But it was usually a mistake to understand Carter too quickly. If we examine his words more closely, Carter was drawing a clear line between himself and Scheer—and, by implication, all those who didn't live up to his moral standards. At the very least, Carter was reminding us that he has a straight line to God: ". . . and God forgives me." He generously announces that, with God's help, he won't condemn the rest of us, just because he's pure and we're a bunch of fornicators, but he leaves no doubt that to condemn us would be a reasonable act for a lesser man, or that the thought had crossed his mind.

It seems to me that this outburst, which was widely accepted as a statement of humility, is one of the most self-serving pronouncements I can imagine. The national uproar over Carter's "lust"—endless sermons and editorial cartoons and pious posturing—was as absurd as it was devastating. Carter's problem was pride, not lust, as he well knew.

In retrospect, it is difficult to overstate the impact of the *Playboy* interview, not only on the campaign but on Carter's presidency. It destroyed his lead, soured his press relations, threw him on the defensive and his campaign into chaos, and probably cost him the big electoral victory he had expected. Moreover, Carter's remarks first raised the possibility to millions of voters that he might be a bit too different, too strange, for them to be comfortable with for four or eight years. The honeymoon was over. Scheer had indeed goaded Carter into self-revelation, and his prideful outburst was the turning point of his political career.

We flew back to Plains Monday night so Carter could prepare for the first debate with Ford, in Philadelphia on Thursday. The furor over the *Playboy* interview was sweeping the nation. There had not been any burning issues in the campaign, but now there was an issue that everyone could understand: our pious candidate had made himself look silly. Caddell reported that by Tuesday night we had fallen from ten points ahead to even. By Wednesday night we were behind.

Two weeks earlier, in the memo I wrote Carter but never delivered, I warned, "The pressures are going to get very tough in the next few weeks, and unless the people on the plane like and respect one another it's going to be a long and painful eight weeks."

In the aftermath of the *Playboy* interview, my prediction came true. When you have a big lead, everyone loves everyone, but when you fall behind people lash out and look for scapegoats. One night that week, Greg and Marie had the staff over for dinner at their little house outside Americus. It was a pretty dismal affair. Jody was grumbling about the press even more than usual.

Jody was under terrible pressure, because Carter blamed the press secretary for persuading him to grant the *Playboy* interview. Jody was particularly furious with the way ABC's Sam Donaldson had handled the story and was saying how he would get even with Donaldson. He would be unfailingly polite to him, but would slowly cut him off from the news. "He thinks we have to suffer for our sins," Jody said, "but he doesn't have to suffer for his."

When the party broke up, I caught a ride back to the Best Western with Jody and two of his assistants. He was grumbling about what a son of a bitch Bob Scheer was. I said I'd spoken to ABC's Judy Woodruff, who'd been dating Scheer, and she said he was upset about the harm the interview was doing Carter. Jody bitterly rejected that possibility and went on to say that that goddamn Scheer even had the audacity to say, on the *Today Show*, that Carter had been trying to win his favor with his remarks about lust and shacking up.

"Well, maybe he was," I said. It was a dumb remark, but I was sick of Jody blaming Donaldson, blaming Scheer, blaming everyone but Carter for Carter's blunder.

"If you think that, maybe you ought to be working for Scheer," Jody shot back.

I let it pass. I didn't want to argue with Jody in front of the others. But back at the motel I walked with him to his room, where I told him, "Jody, I don't care what you think about Scheer, but I don't want you making shitty comments to me."

He responded with a new tirade against Scheer.

I repeated that I didn't appreciate obnoxious comments to me, and he denounced *Playboy* and Scheer some more. We went back and forth like that. At one point I said I was more objective about *Playboy* than he was. "Obviously," he said drily. Objectivity was no virtue in Jody's book.

Jody was stonewalling me, and he was one of the world's great stonewallers. He didn't want to make things worse, but he wasn't going to back down either. I restated my case, that the *Playboy* disaster was Carter's own fault, and in any event I didn't intend to take any crap from him, and he restated his, which in one version was, "We've been fucked and if you've been fucked you at least ought to admit it."

This could have gone on all night, so I said, "OK, I've made my point," and departed.

Carter spent the next day getting ready for his debate with Ford, and the *Playboy* controversy was probably the reason he prepared so poorly. Jerry Rafshoon had suggested that he meet with his senior staff for an intensive question-and-answer session, as we knew Ford was doing. Carter refused, but agreed to talk over the debate with his staff. Greg asked who he wanted in the meeting, and Carter wrote down five names: Greg, Jody,

Stu, Caddell, Rafshoon. But when this quintet went to see Carter they found him in no mood for advice, so Rafshoon gave a summary of their ideas and they withdrew. That nonbriefing, with the ghost of *Playboy* hanging over it, plus Carter's underestimation of Ford, led to the disaster the next night.

We had a bit of comic relief in Philadelphia the day of the first debate. Norman Mailer had called me in Plains the day before. His piece for the *New York Times Magazine* would be out on Sunday, he explained, and coming on top of the *Playboy* interview it might cause a problem for us. He wouldn't be specific but promised to get a copy to me as soon as possible. The magazine reached me in Philadelphia, and I soon saw the problem. When Norman questioned Carter about morality, censorship, and dirty talk, the candidate had said impatiently, "I don't care if people say 'fuck.'" The *Times* printed that as "I don't care if people say ———," but when reporters called the paper a spokesman was helpfully explaining that "———" meant *fuck*.

I showed the article to Jody and Greg, and we groaned a bit, but our consensus was that, after the *Playboy* disaster, this wouldn't matter much.

We flew to Texas, where the burning controversy was Carter's declaration to *Playboy* that "I don't think I would ever take on the same frame of mind that Nixon or Johnson did—lying, cheating and distorting the truth."

In the real world, of course, everyone knew that Lyndon Johnson lied, cheated, and distorted the truth—it was part of his charm. But he was a folk hero in Texas, and his widow was reportedly outraged. When we arrived in Houston, Carter was met by reporters, to whom he gave this amazing explanation:

"The unfortunate thing about the magazine interview was the post-interview statement about President Johnson, which completely distorts my feelings about him. . . . After the interview was over, there was a summary made and unfortunately it equated" his feelings about Nixon and Johnson. He added, "It was an analysis that was made at the completion of the interview. . . . [T]he unfortunate juxtaposition of these two names in the *Playboy* article grossly misrepresents the way I feel about Johnson."

Those tortured remarks were at best misleading. No one had distorted or summarized his remarks. He said what he said and *Playboy* had it on tape. Needless to say, his evasions became the day's big story. The candidate who promised to never tell a lie had told a whopper. I think Carter's confused self-justification was less a lie, however, than a breakdown. God only knows what inner torment Carter was suffering by then. This proud, self-righteous man had somehow used his religion to make himself a laughingstock and perhaps to blow the election. I think when he made those remarks he was very close to the edge.

In San Diego that evening, I was sitting in the bar of the Royal Inn Hotel with Barbara Howar and Mary Fifield, waiting for Marty Schram to join us for dinner. Barbara was on the campaign both as a journalist and as one of Jerry Rafshoon's romantic interests. Mary was a talented young woman who'd recently joined our press staff. When Marty didn't turn up, I went to look for him and discovered that he and other reporters had been summoned to Carter's room for an off-the-record talk.

I slipped in and listened. Carter was straddling a coffee table, and reporters filled all the chairs and were sitting on the floor. Carter protested that negative press coverage was killing his campaign and asked what he could do to improve things. The reporters replied that they could not be in the position of advising him, but were quick to assert that his own gaffes and misleading statements were the real problem.

The meeting accomplished little—perhaps it cleared the air a bit—but I found it quite remarkable. By then Carter loathed those reporters, and for him to go to them hat in hand was a measure of how desperate he was. When that meeting provided no miracle cure, he proceeded to follow his natural instincts and see less and less of the national media for the rest of the campaign.

Even before the *Playboy* interview, many reporters had suspected lust in the candidate's heart. "Come on, Pat," they would say, "off the record, do you think he's ever played around?" I would reply that while I think anything at all is possible where sex is concerned, I assumed that a combination of religion, a good marriage, and fear of exposure had kept him in line.

"Ah, but that'll change once he's president," one reporter told me.

I asked what she meant.

"Well, he's never known a *sophisticated* woman," the lady said, and I thought we had a volunteer for the assignment.

Our next stop was the famous San Diego Zoo, where Carter managed to get his picture taken holding a snake aloft, to the delight of reporters who'd always considered him a snake-handler. Carter also put the knife to his host, Jerry Brown, by innocently remarking to reporters that he'd sure been surprised when the governor told him he'd never visited this wonderful zoo before.

As we returned to Georgia for the weekend, everyone's nerves were frayed. I got into a tiff with Jody, who hadn't liked a piece I'd written for Carter for the op-ed page of the New York *Times*. I barely restrained myself from telling Jody that I'd been writing for the New York *Times* before he'd ever heard of it. It was like that for the duration. Too many egos confined in too small a space. Jim Fallows, being younger and less philosophical than I, would get even madder at Jody and the candidate than I did. Jim and I would joke darkly about the Secret Service's elaborate anti-assassin programs: The real danger, we said, was that Carter would be flung from a hotel window by a deranged speechwriter.

When we arrived back in Georgia, Peanut One landed at Albany and let off Carter and most of the staff and media, who proceeded to Plains or Americus. Then the plane flew to Atlanta for servicing, carrying whoever wanted to go along. On these flights, the inmates took over the asylum. The booze flowed freely, and we took turns sitting in Carter's chair and calling our wives and/or girlfriends on the air-to-ground phone. That night, when we landed, Jody drove me to Ann's apartment in his battled old VW bug. I was furious at Carter about some rebuff.

"I don't *need* this shit," I raged. "If you can find somebody else who can do this job better, feel free!"

Jody shrugged. "Anybody else we got would have the same problems with him you have," he said, ever the realist.

The next morning, Ann and I flew home to see Laura. We spent the evening with a friend who had heard that the campaign's problem was that Jody didn't know how to handle the national media.

I found myself in the unlikely position of defending Jody. "He does the job as well as anyone could," I insisted. "Don't blame him. Win or lose, this campaign is all Carter. The rest of us are just along for the ride."

My neighbor and I clashed again when I mentioned that my friend Keith Stroup, the founder of the National Organization for the Reform of Marijuana Law, had asked me to be an honorary sponsor (with Garry Trudeau and Christie Hefner) of a cocktail party at NORML's annual convention in December.

My neighbor was outraged. I was working for the next president, he said, and I couldn't let my name be associated with marijuana reform. Stroup was only trying to use me.

I laughed. "I've used him as a good source of dope," I said. "Anyway, I told him not to announce it until after the election. It won't matter then."

My neighbor continued to protest. I was headed for the White House, he said, but I could blow it if I hung around with the likes of Stroup.

I was unmoved. I didn't know where I was headed, but I knew I was too old to change my friends for political reasons, the White House notwithstanding.

8
WE ALL USED TO BE LIBERALS

On the afternoon of Saturday, October 2, Carter spoke to a coalition of women's groups meeting in Washington, D.C. I had asked Ann to write a first draft, on the assumption that she could deal with our in-house feminists better than I could. The feminists, like the environmentalists, were furious that Carter hadn't delivered "their" speech. But Carter's advisers were in no hurry, because they assumed he had both groups locked up and didn't want to risk offending voters on the other side of the issues. By then, I dreaded going to our headquarters, knowing that angry feminists and eco-freaks would corner me and demand, "Where's our speech?"

Ann gave me what I wanted, a solid, factual draft that promised the women's movement everything on its wish list ("Promise her anything . . ."). I added rhetorical touches and delivered the speech to Carter. Then Ann and I flew home for a visit with Laura.

A problem soon arose. Down in Plains, Greg edited the speech and, among other outrages, cut all mention of the Equal Rights Amendment. I couldn't believe it. If there was anything Carter was committed to, it was the ERA. If he went before those women and didn't mention the ERA, he might not get out alive. I called Greg and raised hell, and he restored one lukewarm plug.

Greg's editing reflected the new, post-*Playboy* caution of the campaign. We clearly didn't need more controversy or off-the-wall remarks, but to back off from the ERA was not caution, it was madness. I assumed that Greg had edited the speech at Carter's request because he was starting to see me as a liberal crazy who might slip some bombshell past him. I accepted this philosophically. History can decide who was the crazy on this campaign.

Ann and I met Carter's plane in Washington and urged him to make a strong statement on the ERA. When we arrived at the hall, I was introduced to Gloria Steinem and other feminist leaders. As we talked, Jody passed by.

"That's Jody Powell," one woman said.

"He's attractive," another noted.

"He is now," a third said coolly. "But he won't be in ten years."

The speech began well. I had urged Carter to extemporize about the women in his family, and he did: his mother's stint with the Peace Corps, Rosalynn's job in a beauty parlor as a girl, and her mother's working as a seamstress after her husband died.

Encouraged by cheers from the women (cheers inspired in part by three plugs for the ERA), Carter began to wing it. He was trying to say that Americans are fair and that when they understand the ERA they will support it.

"I believe our country and its people are still idealistic, and filled with a sense of brotherhood and compassion and love," he declared.

Brotherhood?

The women began to boo, hiss, and jeer.

Carter quickly added, "Brotherhood and sisterhood!"

He returned to the safety of my text, which concluded: "I have, as you know, an eight-year-old daughter, Amy. I love her very much. I don't get to see her often. I hope when Amy becomes an adult she can be just as sure of becoming a doctor as a nurse, just as sure of being a lawyer as a secretary, and that she can be just as sure of becoming president as a president's daughter."

Ann and I listened with tears in our eyes. I'd written that for our daughter, although it worked for Carter and Amy too.

The speech had gone well, and some good coverage, to remind America's women that we loved them, wouldn't have hurt us any. In fact, it won precious little coverage. The New York *Times* buried the story, and the Washington *Post* didn't carry a word—strange, since it had a woman publisher and presumably cared about women's issues. In part, the poor coverage probably had to do with the early deadlines for the Sunday papers. More important, October 2 was the day that Secretary of Agriculture Earl Butz's remarks about black men came to light—"All they want is loose shoes, tight pussy, and a warm place to shit"—and his rhetoric, not mine, won the next day's headlines.

The Best Western Motel, Americus, Georgia, October

My room contained two double beds. I slept in one and piled speeches on the other. Hundreds of unsolicited speeches were pouring in from leading Democratic thinkers like Jack Valenti, from former Cabinet members and would-be Cabinet members, and from concerned citizens across the nation. I had no interest in reading them, either for pleasure or plagiarism—this campaign was going to sink or swim with *my* speeches. So I would stack them on my extra bed until they began to overflow onto the floor, when I would finally toss them in the wastebasket, after first removing any paperclips that were attached. You never knew when you'd need a paperclip.

Outside my door, the motel was besieged by would-be officeholders. I had to bolt from my room to my car to escape their importunings. Once, at the urging of the motel's manager, I met with some decent, desperate people whose loved one was a political prisoner somewhere in Central America and who could not believe that a powerful man like myself could not free him. The motel manager and I were in frequent contact, because the campaign owed him thousands of dollars in back rent and he had the idea that I could fix that, too.

The Best Western Motel, a Sunday morning in October

The speechwriter has had it with the press secretary. All he asks out of life is to land one punch on his smug face. After that, he realizes, the press secretary will murder him, being younger, bigger, stronger, and meaner, but the crazed wordsmith no longer cares. Just one punch!

The speechwriter enters the motel office to confront his nemesis. He is startled to find not only the press secretary and the pollster, but the press secretary's admirable wife. He cannot attack the man in front of this good woman, so he leans against the doorway, scowling, poised to strike.

The pollster, a bulky young man called Pat, is on the phone, getting the latest numbers from his staff. With these numbers, he and the press secretary are to brief a roomful of waiting reporters.

"Goddamn," the pollster begins to sputter. "Goddamn, goddamn!"

All the eyes are fixed on the befuddled pollster. Clearly, something is happening. Whether good or bad is uncertain. Finally the pollster puts down the phone and a smile breaks across his great moon of a face.

"We're pulling away," he whispers. "*Playboy* is over. The economy is taking hold. It's happening everywhere. We're pulling away!"

Suddenly the room is filled with cheers, grins, handshakes, backslaps. "We can get ourselves a couple of straw hats," the press secretary tells the pollster. "We can dance into the briefing room with the old softshoe. We can say: 'I'm Jody,' 'I'm Pat,' 'We're here to entertain you!'"

The press secretary breaks into a graceful softshoe. The speechwriter almost breaks into tears. They were going to win, and nothing else mattered.

On October 4, Carter spoke to the National Conference of Catholic Charities, in Denver. These were the good, liberal, social-worker Catholics, and I wrote one of his most liberal speeches. We opened with this jibe at the opposition:

"We've been governed too long by people who are isolated from the realities of life in America. Our leaders have spent too many years wandering through Washington's quiet corridors of power, or strolling the plush green fairways of privilege."

The "plush green fairways" line played off charges that Ford had accepted favors from a lobbyist who was also one of his golfing buddies. That was about as dirty as we got in 1976. Compared to the character assassination of campaigns to come, we were innocent as babes. Stu had a sinister-looking fellow on his staff who was said to be in charge of "negative research," but I don't think I ever met him.

Our Catholic desk had prepared a first draft of the speech that used the buzzword "pluralism" about twenty times. My draft used the word maybe three times. Carter scribbled in the margin: "Pat—eliminate 'pluralism'— I don't know what it is—substitute what it means. JC." I loved that; at his best, Carter had no tolerance for jargon.

It was a good speech, given before a wildly enthusiastic audience, yet Carter raced through it impatiently. I think his mind was on our next stop, San Francisco, where two days later he would debate Ford for the second time. He had been casual about the first debate; this time he was out for blood. When we talked about a closing statement, he said grimly, "Make it tough—no bullshit!"

Carter didn't so much win the second debate as Ford lost it with his muddled remarks about the Soviets not dominating Eastern Europe. But the next day Carter said in a stump speech that Ford had sounded "brainwashed," so the story reverted from "Dumb Jerry" to "Mean Jimmy." Still, the stories on Ford's blunder, like our *Playboy* flap, went on relentlessly, day after day after day. You almost felt sorry for Ford and his people; you knew what it was like, and it wasn't fun.

In South Bend, on Sunday, October 10, a wire-service story appeared about our campaign manual. The manual contained only routine advance-man procedures—how to inflate crowds and stage media events and the like—but the reporter made it sound Machiavellian in the extreme. As luck would have it, Carter was attending Sunday school that morning at a school for mentally retarded children near the Notre Dame campus. We feared the visit would inspire stories that we were using retarded kids to gain publicity. We therefore decreed there would be no media at the service. Normally, at least a pool reporter would have gone with Carter.

I went along, and to escape the heat and the reporters I slipped into the service. Carter was sitting in the middle of a schoolroom, wearing a gray suit, surrounded by about twenty children. Greg, who knew something about retardation because Marie had taught retarded kids, told me these were severe cases. Throughout the service, the children moaned, screamed, drooled, wandered aimlessly about the room, or stared vacantly into space. By the time their chorus began singing "Jesus Loves Me," I was slumped in the back of the room, thinking of my own two perfect children, going to pieces as inconspicuously as possible.

Carter sat there amid the bedlam, smiling serenely, seeming to enjoy himself. I tried to understand how he could accept this scene so calmly. He had visited a lot of mental institutions, of course. Moreover, his religion surely helped: He believed Jesus truly does love these children and will wash away their ills in a world to come.

As I watched Carter, I thought: This is it, this is where he fills his tank. He draws strength from these children as surely as Jerry Ford draws his from playing eighteen holes with Bob Hope at Pebble Beach. This is why he does it, to gain the power to help these children. And I thought: I am sick of this man, I am sick of all this madness, but I must do whatever I can because it matters. It really does matter.

Glimpses of the press secretary

The end was near, the polls were bad, and tempers were short. One day I mentioned Greg to Jody, and Jody snapped, "A suckass, that's what he's gettin' to be!" The reason for his outburst, I learned, was that Greg had conspired with Carter to elude the media after church one recent Sunday in Plains. Jody was angry because he caught hell from the reporters if Carter got out of their sight. (What if somebody shot him and they missed the story?) Greg's position was that he worked for Carter, not for Jody.

One day in mid-October, Jody asked me to write a statement on the twentieth anniversary of the Hungarian uprising. I thought about those Hungarians challenging Soviet tanks with rocks and sticks, and wrote a pretty good statement. I gave it to Jody. Later I received an urgent call from Atlanta, asking where the statement was. Ask Jody, I said, but Jody denied any knowledge of its whereabouts. Eventually, his secretary found the statement, deep in his briefcase, but it was too late to matter.

One day, near the end, Jody and I were in the front cabin of Peanut One and I said something about his role in the White House.

"I may not be in the White House," he grumbled. "I don't think I can take those assholes back there any longer." He gestured toward the rear of the plane, where our friends the reporters sat.

I was stunned. Was Jody starting to crack? I had cracked a long time back, and I feared the candidate was congenitally half-cracked, but I thought of Jody as a pillar of sanity aboard this flying madhouse. If he couldn't take it any longer, we were in trouble.

For Carter's October 14 appearance at the Liberal Party dinner in New York, I wrote a speech critical of the stereotypes so dear to both liberals and conservatives. It said in part:

"In domestic affairs, too many conservative stereotypes have portrayed liberals as fuzzy-headed and wasteful, and conservatives on the other hand as realistic and efficient. And liberals sometimes see themselves as overflowing with the compassion that the hardhearted conservatives always lack.

"I reject both stereotypes. . . . They bear little resemblance to the real world, in which we find a lot of people who combine both compassion and competence, who have, in Adlai Stevenson's phrase, both warm hearts and cool heads.

"Also, our national foreign policy dialogue has been too often distorted by clichés and polarization. The code words have been 'soft' and 'tough.' We've suffered enough in this country because some Presidents and their advisers have felt it necessary to prove their supposed toughness by pursuing rash and ultimately tragic policies.

"A strong nation, like a strong person, can afford to be gentle, firm, thoughtful, and restrained. It can afford to extend a helping hand to others. It is a weak nation, like a weak person, that must behave with bluster and boasting and rashness and other signs of insecurity."

Our sermon didn't satisfy the redoubtable Bella Abzug, who cornered me after the speech and roared, "What does he think he's doing, coming to New York and not talking about the urban crisis?"

She went on like that, nonstop, as I became more and more angry—not just at Abzug, but at the multitudes who were forever telling me what was wrong with everything Carter said. Finally I broke into her tirade with the four-letter word most likely to offend her:

"*Lady* . . ." I began ominously.

"DON'T CALL ME LADY!"

"Lady," I persisted, "do you know why Carter's going to be the next president?"

"Why?"

"Because he says what he damn well pleases!"

After that we had a good talk.

After the election, James Reston wrote in the New York *Times* that Carter had not delivered a single memorable speech during the campaign. For what it's worth, I thought Carter delivered five memorable speeches. The Martin Luther King speech. The acceptance speech. The Town Hall Forum speech. His basic stump speech, considered in its entirety, as it evolved over two years. That was his greatest speech, the one that did as much as anything to make him president. The fifth speech on my list, and the least-known of them, was delivered at a memorial dinner for Congressman Jerry Litton and his family on October 15 in Kansas City, Missouri. Litton and his wife and two children had died in the crash of a private plane ten weeks earlier, on the very night he had won the Democratic nomination for the Senate. Litton was a farmer/businessman/politician like Carter. They'd met only once, but afterward Carter told Rosalynn he'd met a man who could be president. Litton, for his part, was one of the first members of Congress to endorse Carter.

At Carter's request, I had Bill Keel prepare a detailed memo on Litton's life. Because Carter had a major speech on crime in Detroit earlier that day, he had only a couple of hours on the plane to study the memo and prepare his remarks, which he delivered from notes. Nonetheless, he gave an extremely personal and moving tribute. I think Carter identified not only with Litton's life but with his death. He knew that his own plane might have gone down in all his months of hedgehopping. I think Carter wanted to deliver for Litton the kind of tribute he would have wanted for himself. To an extent he was talking about his own life as well as Litton's.

He spoke about the importance of a politician's family:

"Jerry Litton was blessed by his family, as you well know. His mother and father, and his wife and children, they were a team. And I know the benefit in that. Because a lot of times in politics, as you well know, it's a lonely thing. Particularly when you are just getting started—running for Congress or running for governor or running for president.

"Most of the time, in those early stages, when you say, 'I want to be Congressman of the Sixth District,' and then you walk away, you know there are a lot of jokes and smirking, and you feel very humble. To walk in front of a service station and talk to five people and say, 'Would you vote for me for Congress?' And quite often you feel that you are not quite worthy in their eyes. You think more of yourself, but you're sure that they don't think you're qualified to go off to Washington.

"But the family that's there—your wife and others who have confidence in you—always provide a base, a solid base, that's unshakable. You can take the ups and downs, endorsements and endorsements of your opponents, favorable newspaper editorials and those that are very critical, success in a speech and a speech that fumbles. And with the bad editorials, and the endorsements of your opponent, and the speeches that fail, it's always great to come home to a wife who is an equal partner in the process."

He tried to define his standard of excellence:

"I think you see clearly that Jerry Litton's successes were not accidents. He owed his success to his friends who had confidence in him. He never betrayed that confidence, or the commitment to principles that never changed. He owed his success to a great exuberance. He didn't trudge through life, plodding one step at a time. He ran through life with a great happiness and a joy. He never let a potential obstacle deter him. In fact, sometimes I think he welcomed it. The tough battles, the uphill fights, challenged him and let him draw on the strength that came from the support of his family and friends.

"That is the kind of politics that ought to exist more often in our country. Tonight we come to pay tribute to him. I'm saddened by it. I called his parents as soon as I heard about the tragedy. But tonight is not a time of sorrow. We've been through that sorrowful period. God's blessed us by having had a chance to know Jerry Litton. Or to know about him. And I hope that the few remarks that I've made tonight will impress on each one of us, including myself, some of those unchanging characteristics of human potential that should inspire us all. To be a little better. To set a slightly higher standard in our own lives. Not to be satisfied with mediocrity, but excellence. Not to be concerned only about the problems of our country, but to recognize its present and potential greatness."

Near the end, Carter said:

"We don't ever know what causes tragedies, or what God's purpose is on earth. But we do know that our own life here is transient. All of us. But what we leave behind is important. And although Jerry Litton may not have his own family here to carry on in generations to come, he has us and other people who knew him, who can maybe extract something, large or small, from him, and let it be part of our own lives to pass on from one year to another."

Bill Keel had suggested that Carter end the speech with the lines from *Romeo and Juliet* that Robert Kennedy had used in his eulogy for John Kennedy at the 1964 Democratic convention. I thought those lines too sentimental for Carter, but I was wrong. After noting that "I'm going to take some poetic license and express it in the plural," he closed with Shakespeare's words:

> When they shall die
> Take them and cut them out in little stars
> And they shall make the heavens so fine
> That all the world will be in love with night.

After that, Carter didn't say "Thank you" or "Goodnight." He simply stepped back, overcome with emotion, handed his notes to Litton's mother, and left the hall as Litton's family and friends sprang to their feet. There were few dry eyes in the room. If there's anyone else in recent American politics who could have produced and delivered a finer eulogy under those difficult circumstances, he or she has escaped my attention.

The speech was not reported outside of Missouri, of course. That was the night of the Mondale-Dole debate, and it was the next day's story.

As we flew back to Georgia the following day, Carter came out of his cabin and moved down the aisle, greeting staff and press. Bill Keel was sitting with me, and Carter told him he appreciated the excellent memo he'd given him on Jerry Litton.

"My pleasure," Bill said with a big grin. He didn't know that I'd asked Carter to thank him for his help.

"Pat's been talkin' you up to me."

Bill, a man Carter's age, blushed at the compliment. "He's my friend," he said.

"He's a good man," Carter said, grinning. "We're learnin' each other."

That was an expression that both Carter and Rosalynn used. Not that they were learning about something, but simply that they were learning it, clearly a more difficult task. I was glad Carter thought we were learning each other. I wondered if there'd ever be time to complete the process.

On October 21, Carter spoke at the Al Smith Dinner in New York, a traditional highlight of presidential campaigns. Ford also spoke, but he left before we arrived. Carter and I had discussed the speech on the plane a few nights earlier. The audience would largely be wealthy, conservative Catholics who were active in local and national politics. "I want to tell them there are serious issues to be discussed in this campaign and it's time we addressed them," he told me. I thought I knew what he was driving at. Catholics had given him a hard time on abortion, from the bishops who'd met with him and then sandbagged him to the right-to-life shock troops who'd dogged our campaign for months. I could imagine how sick he must be of this. Abortion was a phony issue, since his position and Ford's were virtually identical.

Emboldened by a few drinks, I said, "What you're trying to say is, 'I'm a tough guy and you're tough guys and let's stop playing fuckaround.'"

The candidate flashed a tight little smile. "That's right," he said.

That was not the ideal message to deliver, however. The Al Smith Dinner was traditionally a light, nonpartisan affair, where both candidates told jokes and spoke in generalities. Al Smith had been a fighting liberal in his youth, then an embittered conservative in old age. Every four years the Democratic candidate praises the young Al and the Republican hails the mature Smith of later years.

I gave Carter a draft that began with a dozen jokes, paid tribute to young Al, then talked about the family and the New York fiscal crisis. On the flight to New York, we went over my draft. He'd cut the jokes down to three. The first played off Ford's habit of forgetting what town he was in: "It's great to be here in Chicago." But upon arrival we found that Ford had used a similar line, deftly making a joke on himself, so we had to cut ours.

The next joke was mine: "After twenty-two months of campaigning, I won't say I always know where I am, but when I don't I've at least learned to avoid the issue."

I was speaking to Ted Sorensen again and I'd gotten the third joke from him. Sorensen, who had written Kennedy's celebrated speech to this dinner in 1960, had Carter saying he'd promised Cardinal Cooke that "if I ever give another interview on the biblical sins of pride and lust, it will be to a reporter from *Our Sunday Visitor*." That echoed Kennedy's 1960 quip that for the *Wall Street Journal* to criticize Richard Nixon was like the *Observatore Romano* criticizing the Pope.

Carter proceeded to another passage I'd used from Sorensen, one that pointed out parallels between himself and Al Smith: "We honor tonight a man who ran for President without having previously served in Washington, whose only previous high office was governor of his state, who was criticized for his religion and his accent . . ." et cetera.

After that, Carter had added two lines of his own:

"Unfortunately, in 1928, the Republican candidate won, and the next year we entered the Great Depression.

"I think the result will be different this year."

Perhaps I should have caught those lines when he showed them to me, but I didn't. Carter had no sooner spoken them than boos echoed across the vast Waldorf-Astoria ballroom. In theory these were boos for Carter having made a blatantly partisan statement; more likely they came from partisans who were looking for an excuse to jeer. If so, we served one up on a platter.

As Carter continued, he began to edit out lines that might possibly be seen as partisan. It was a neat performance, but it didn't matter. The next day's news showed him being booed at the Al Smith Dinner, not exactly what we'd wanted.

We were in Williamsburg, Virginia, on October 22 for the third debate. In the dining room of the Williamsburg Inn, I ran into my friend David Kennerly, who was President Ford's White House photographer. David and I had met two years earlier when we both traveled with Vice President Ford—I was on a *New York Times Magazine* assignment, he was working for *Time*—as Ford spent an Easter vacation playing golf at the Pebble Beach and Thunderbird courses and gamely defending the doomed Nixon before Republican audiences.

David and I had had some adventures on that trip and we'd kept in touch. He had taken the photo of me, on the White House lawn, for the jacket of *The President's Mistress.* I was delighted to see him in Williamsburg, but he was having lunch with some Ford strategists who weren't delighted to meet me, so we went to another table. David was very fond of Ford (who, indeed, I'd found personally likable), and he was as sure that Ford would win as I was that Carter would. We agreed that whoever backed the winning candidate would buy the other dinner, then we returned to the rival camps.

Carter had lost support among women because of the *Playboy* interview. It was decided that Rosalynn would campaign with him for a few days, in hopes of network footage showing a happily married candidate. She joined us in Williamsburg and was along for our stop in Alexandria, Virginia.

Carter's support was far below what it should have been in the Northern Virginia suburbs, because thousands of federal employees feared that Carter's promised government reorganization would cost them their jobs. In fact, he had always stressed that jobs would be reduced by attrition.

The obvious solution was for Carter to explain about attrition at his big outdoor rally in Alexandria. But we feared that if he did, the media would say he was waffling on government reorganization. The price of wooing bureaucrats in Northern Virginia might have been another round of "Carter Flip-flops" stories.

Carter, Rosalynn, Jody, Greg, and I debated the problem at length and reached a compromise: Rosalynn would explain in *her* speech that Carter's reorganization would not put bureaucrats on the street. She did that, but it was a wasted effort; the media didn't care what the candidate's wife said about government reorganization.

What I remember about Rosalynn's speech that morning was not what she said but the passion with which she spoke. She'd campaigned so long and hard, the end was near, and all her pride and hunger and anxiety came pouring out. It was an electrifying performance. For the first time I saw what Hamilton meant when he said she wanted the White House even worse than Jimmy did. When Rosalynn finished, Carter's speech was absurdly anticlimactic. It was like sending John Denver onstage after Tina Turner.

Back in Georgia that weekend, Greg heard that Bob Dylan wanted to do something for the campaign. Greg and I were overjoyed. We imagined Carter and Dylan sharing a stage, singing a duet of "The Times They Are A-Changing," whereupon a great outpouring of the freak vote would sweep us to victory. Greg called Hamilton in Atlanta to tell him the good news. To our dismay, Ham wasn't sure the candidate should ally himself with Dylan at this late and delicate moment. Greg called Carter, who reported that he'd just been listening to Dylan's new album and he thought it'd be great to appear with him. Finally, with a call to someone in the Dylan camp, we learned it was all a mistake—the singer was in Europe.

As the campaign entered its final week, I didn't expect to write any more speeches. Carter would speak mostly at big outdoor rallies, and Jody, Greg, and I agreed he had neither the time nor the energy to deal with new material. Nor did he have the desire. In those final days he was returning more and more to the themes of his early stump speeches. He had been campaigning a long time, he would tell audiences. When he started he didn't have much money or support, but he'd traveled across America and gone to beauty shops and union halls and farmers' markets and talked to ordinary people and learned their concern that America had lost its way. He was using phrases I'd first heard in Florida fourteen months before, and hadn't heard often that fall. Watching, listening, I thought of a line by T. S. Eliot: "In my end is my beginning."

I think the campaign had become utterly personal to him. I usually felt that if a speech didn't make the network news it was wasted. But I think he'd given up on the media, decided it would never report his message, only his blunders. In those final weeks, he was speaking to each audience as if it alone could make the difference. Perhaps it could. Perhaps the Jerry Litton speech could swing Missouri if Litton's friends were moved to an extra effort. With the election so close, who could say that one passionate speech might not sway the votes that would carry the state that would make the difference?

It was an awesome sight. He had the money and machinery of a great political party behind him, yet none of that seemed to matter. All that mattered was this one exhausted man, standing before his fellow Americans, telling them about his wife and family, asking their help.

On the afternoon of Wednesday, October 27, we were flying to Pittsburgh, where Carter would speak to the Allegheny County Democratic Dinner, when Greg summoned me to Carter's compartment. Carter was asleep, on a bunk behind a curtain, but Greg and Jody were at his table and wanted to talk about the speech that night.

"He's tired," Jody said. "He was rambling today. We think you ought to give him something to work from tonight."

Greg and Jody proposed a three-part speech. First he would say he had traveled around America and seen the problems, the unemployment, the disillusion. But, he would say, he had also seen courage, hope, a determination not to give up. Finally he would close with the "I see an America" litany. That sounded good to me, and I went to work.

I wrote standing up at the back of the plane, with my typewriter atop a cabinet, until we landed. On the ride into Pittsburgh, I worked on the press bus, pausing every few sentences for a swig from Dick Reeves's beer. I finished the speech in my hotel room and took it down the hall to Carter's room.

I found him in jockey shorts and a T-shirt, stretched crossways across the bed, as if he'd thrown himself down and been too tired to straighten out. I said I had the speech but I wouldn't bother him if he was too tired. He said he'd look at it.

I handed him the speech and he put it on the floor, so he could read it without moving, with his head hanging over the edge of the bed. I sat on the sofa and ate strawberries from a basket of fruit. He suggested a few additions and I started to leave. He was still crossways on the bed; he had never looked up.

"Thank you very much, Pat," he whispered.

I was moved that this exhausted man, who literally hadn't the strength to raise his head, had thanked me. It was the most I ever liked him.

An hour later he bounded into the ballroom, waving and smiling, and delivered one of his best speeches of the campaign. He used my draft as a framework, but built on it, putting more of himself into it, always improving it, as I watched in wonder.

In those final days, there was a running debate between those of us—mainly me, Jody, and Greg—who felt we should leave Carter alone, and others, mainly Stu, who were still looking for some new act or pronouncement that would "turn around" this painfully close election. Our side felt there were no more issues, that Carter was the issue, and there was nothing to do but hold on for the ride. We were winning the debate, since what we wanted was also what Carter wanted.

We were so isolated on the plane. Our world extended from Peanut One to the motorcade to the rally to the hotel, and was populated by the candidate, four or five staff people, and a dozen or so reporters. Everything beyond that was a blur. One night, following Carter into a rally in St. Louis as thousands cheered the candidate, I suddenly remembered all those people out there who were counting on us, decent people who cared about America, as I had four years before. But now I was past caring, wanting only for the madness to end.

Yet it was wonderful, too, near the end. There are few experiences more exhilarating than to see tens of thousands of people cheering your candidate, to feel the tide running your way, to think your man will win and you helped this miracle come to pass.

The cities flew by: Erie, Cleveland, Gary, Toledo. There was a nice moment in New Orleans the Saturday morning before the election as we marched through the French Quarter behind a Dixieland band, with Jim Wooten and Eleanor Randolph jitterbugging their way down Royal Street.

From New Orleans, I flew a commercial airline to Fort Worth to see my mother. Carter was going to South Texas that evening, and there was nothing I could do for him there. He spoke Spanish and I didn't. I rejoined the campaign the next morning when he attended services at the University Christian Church, a few blocks from my mother's apartment. I'd attended church there myself as a child.

After church, Jody and I climbed into the same car. When Jody pulled out a cigarette and started fumbling for a light, I tossed him a pack of Hugh Hefner's personalized matches that I'd picked up at the Playboy Mansion a few nights before. Jody was not amused.

Luci Johnson introduced Carter at the rally in Fort Worth that afternoon. Luci can be very charming, but this day she was spitting fire. She talked about her daddy, how he'd loved his country, how he'd spent his life helping people, how he'd always been a loyal Democrat, and she managed to introduce Carter without ever mentioning his name or looking in his direction.

We flew to San Francisco for a rally that would be televised statewide. Jerry Brown introduced Carter and helpfully used up most of the thirty minutes of live TV. We had urged Carter to talk about the environment but he didn't have time. Later, at a rally outside his hotel in Sacramento, he spoke eloquently of the environment, but it didn't matter.

On the flight to California that final Sunday, we heard the first reports about a black minister having been turned away from the Plains Baptist Church. On Monday morning, I stood with a dozen reporters in the lobby of our hotel, watching the morning news. There was the minister of Carter's church, saying something about "niggers." No matter that this minister had tried to integrate the church and he was only quoting someone else. No matter that the black man who'd been turned away was an eccentric and sometime Republican office-seeker. What mattered was that on the day before the election, millions of Americans were seeing a report that seemed to link Carter with southern racism.

The reporters were furious. "You stupid sons of bitches—you've blown it!" were the kindest words they had for us. Incredibly enough, most of them wanted Carter to win, and they thought we should have somehow prevented this fiasco at his church.

I was numb, unable to speak. After six months of certitude, I thought for the first time that we could lose the election. I fled the reporters and chanced upon Stu Eizenstat. Soon I was raving at Stu. My largely incoherent thesis was that if we lost, it wouldn't be because of the Republicans, it would be because of liberals. Our liberal friends at *Playboy* had dealt us a mortal blow. Labor and the Kennedy crowd had supported Carter halfheartedly. That great liberal Gene McCarthy, running as a third-party candidate, might drain off enough votes to cost us the election. And now a black man had stabbed us in the back.

"Fucking liberals!" I raged. "Goddammit, Stu, I used to *be* a liberal!"

Stu had never looked more mournful. "Pat," he said gently, "we all used to be liberals."

On election night, Ann and Laura joined me at the Omni Hotel in Atlanta. Laura and Amy spent the evening racing up and down the hotel corridors with a Secret Service agent chasing after them, while Ann and I watched the returns with other staff people.

At Jody's request, I drafted a victory statement, but I considered it wasted effort. If Carter won, he wouldn't be at a loss for words. I was in and out of the big suite where Carter was watching the returns. It was supposed to be reserved for family and close friends, but eventually there were scores of people milling around. Carter was sitting in front of a big TV set, his eyes glued to the screen, oblivious to the crowd.

The night dragged on, the outcome uncertain. It must have been agonizing for Carter. Three months earlier he'd dreamed of a landslide, a great mandate for change, but a few prideful words to *Playboy* had killed that dream. Now he was waiting to see if two or three closely contested states would give him a narrow victory. Did he already see what that would mean, that his mandate was gone, the bold visions of August were gone, that he would take office as a weak president, never to recapture the summer's momentum?

I managed to have an election-night run-in with Jody. *Newsweek*'s Eleanor Clift collared me in the corridor and said Jody had promised to let her into Carter's suite but he had vanished and she would be in desperate trouble if I didn't help her. Eleanor had started as a secretary in *Newsweek*'s Atlanta bureau and she always seemed a little helpless, particularly when pitted against *Time*'s urbane Stan Cloud. Actually, she was bright and tough and headed for a brilliant career in Washington. I got her into the suite and she huddled in the corner taking notes. When Jody arrived he confronted her, then reminded me, quite correctly, that letting reporters in was his job, not mine.

Still, when I left the suite that night, I made a point to seek out Jody and shake his hand. It seemed like the right thing to do. After Carter's final campaign stop, Jody had said, "I was there for the first one and I was there for the last one, and there's no one else who can say that." Egos aside, you had to respect the guy.

Ann and Laura went to our room and around 2 A.M. I decided to join them. Most of the staff were waiting for the rally downstairs when Carter claimed victory, but I'd seen enough rallies. I went over and knelt by Carter's chair until he noticed me.

"I want to say good-bye, governor," I said. "I'm flying home tomorrow."

Carter, his mind far away, gazed at me blankly for a second, then he took my hand and grinned.

"You're great, Patrick," he said. "You're great."

"It's been a pleasure," I said. I was grinning too. It had been a pleasure, in its way.

I should have quit then, while I was ahead.

9

THE VICTORS

The Carters and most of the staff flew to Plains at dawn on Wednesday morning, as though the campaign still raged on, but my family and I went home. Carter wasn't likely to make any speeches soon and I wanted to sleep in my own bed.

On Thursday morning, on very short notice, I drove to Washington to speak to a luncheon at the National Press Club. Hamilton had promised for months that he would be there, two days after the election, but he backed out the day before and offered me and Pat Caddell as his stand-ins. The woman who introduced us raged at great length about Hamilton's perfidy, then said, in effect, "So here are these two bums he sent in his place."

Pat talked about his polls. I don't remember what I talked about, but the Washington *Post* quoted me as saying that the way I survived the election was always to ignore the polls, which was true enough. During the Q & A session, a reporter asked why Carter never told any jokes during the campaign, and I explained that he had, but that no one ever reported them. As proof, I told his "Fifty dollars!" joke, about the uppity woman and the shy divinity student, which was just dumb enough to crack up a couple of hundred hard-bitten Washington reporters.

That afternoon I was in such a hurry to get home that I was stopped for speeding. The deputy looked at my driver's license, then said, "Why, you're Jimmy Carter's speechwriter! I just heard you on the radio. That's a great joke, about the fifty dollars! Don't you worry about this, Mr. Anderson. We're all proud of you. But there's one little thing you might could do."

I asked what that might be.

"Well, me and my wife would sure appreciate a couple of tickets to the Inaugural Ball."

That evening, finally, I was standing before the fire in our living room, free at last, when the phone rang. It was Rex Granum, Jody's assistant.

"Carter's having a news conference in two hours," he said. "Powell wants you to draft an opening statement."

"That's crazy," I protested. "I'm not there. I don't know what he wants to say. Besides, he shouldn't say anything, just answer their questions."

"I could tell Powell I couldn't find you," Rex suggested.

"No, no, that's a coward's way out," I said. "Look, I'll think about it and call you."

I thought about it. I even sat down at my typewriter. But all that came out was, "I'm glad to see you all and I'll take your questions."

I called Rex's secretary and asked her to pass the word that I didn't think Carter needed an opening statement. Then I returned to my fire, waiting for the other shoe to drop. Soon enough, my phone rang again.

"I thought you were going to give us an opening statement," Jody said.

"I don't think you need one," I told him.

We talked for a while. The gist of what he said was that if he made a request of me on behalf of the president-elect, it was highly desirable that I comply, whether or not I happened to agree with it. The gist of what I said was that it was equally desirable that he make reasonable, not unreasonable, requests of me.

Jody was a highly evolved political creature, someone who almost never said what he was really thinking. Obviously he was as sick of me as I was of him, but beyond that, what was in his mind? Did he really think I was going to write the statement from my home? Or was he already thinking that, with the election won, my services were less urgently needed than they'd been before?

A few days later I received a note from Clark Clifford, whom I'd known when I was working as a journalist:

Dear Pat:

As an American citizen and as a Democrat, I thank you for the splendid contribution you made to Governor Carter's victory. It would be very comforting to me to know that you would be a member of the new administration.

Clifford's note reminded me of something he once said to me about Harry Truman's White House staff: "We'd have died for him." I think he meant that literally. Not many of those who worked for Jimmy Carter would say the same.

The Carter "transition office" was located in the gloomy old Health, Education, and Welfare building at the foot of Capitol Hill. Years before, when I first arrived in Washington, I had an office there. I hated that place. It was a prison, except the prisoners were bureaucrats, measuring out their lives in coffee breaks. To return there, even as part of Carter's conquering army, was profoundly depressing.

We had the fifth floor. Out in the corridors, desperate people clutching résumés tried to break past the guards. Inside, our people fought for offices with a view of the Capitol or the Mall. I went there once and didn't return for two weeks.

I spent several weeks editing a book of Carter's speeches. Back on October 13, I had given Carter a memo suggesting such a collection. I said I thought he could command an advance of $25,000 to $50,000 from a major publisher and suggested that he employ my agent, Sterling Lord, to handle the sale. I explained that Sterling would receive the standard 10 percent commission.

We were talking at Carter's house, busy with several things, so I put my memo on the table and suggested he read it later. Three days later, on the plane, I hadn't heard from him, so I mentioned the book idea in another memo. He wrote back: "I saw it—Good idea—Proceed. J."

Thus empowered, I asked Sterling Lord to put the idea to several publishers as soon as the election was won. The best offer, $50,000, came from Michael Korda at Simon & Schuster, my editor on *The President's Mistress*. I reported this to Carter on November 8 and began assembling all known copies of his speeches.

At the outset, Carter grumbled to someone, "I hope Pat includes what I said, and not just what he wrote." He misunderstood my intent. I wanted the book to embody the best of Carter, the often eloquent and inspiring speaker who, against all odds, had literally talked the nation into making him its leader.

I began with his Georgia inaugural and some of his speeches as governor, such as the one to the Lions about his "inner urge" to help the poor. I included all or part of the best 1976 campaign speeches, as well as excerpts from interviews, news conferences, and the debates with Ford. Of some sixty speeches and statements that I included, I had worked on about twenty. The speech collection was a labor of love. It was, as I told someone, Jimmy without the crap.

Carter called on November 15 and asked why he needed a literary agent. I said again that a good agent would more than justify his 10 percent, but Carter was dubious. Soon Bob Lipshutz called. Bob was a big, homely, soft-spoken Atlanta lawyer who was Carter's friend and campaign treasurer. He gently informed me that Carter didn't want to use my agent. "Bob, I submitted a plan to him and the agent was part of the plan and he *approved* it," I protested. But Lipshutz said Carter was "adamant" about the "principle" of not using an agent. I gathered that Carter wanted Lipshutz to handle the book deal, as he had on *Why Not the Best?*

I understood the problem. As Carter saw it, some slick New York agent had simply made a few phone calls and now wanted $5,000 of an honest peanut-farmer's hard-earned money. But I was in an awkward position. Sterling had acted in good faith, on my verbal request, and now Carter was backing out.

Sterling and Lipshutz talked several times. The lawyer insisted I had overstepped my authority. Finally Sterling, tiring of the dispute, said he didn't want anything from Carter. "I'm sorry I voted for the son of a bitch," he told me.

On December 10, Carter's office sent me a bunch of my old memos and speech drafts. Among them was my original proposal for the book of speeches. Carter had written "ok" by various points in the memo, but had written "no" by the proposal that he use my agent. But he never *returned* that memo. Three days later, he had written "Proceed" on my second memo, and I'd taken that as an endorsement of my entire proposal. The whole mess had been an honest misunderstanding. I sent Carter yet another memo, explaining what had happened. He didn't reply, and I knew he would blame me, not himself, for the fiasco.

I went to Atlanta in early December to find some of Carter's early speeches in the state archives. Then I flew back to Washington with Carter. He approved my outline for the speech collection, pointed out a few I'd missed, and, when I asked, told me to include the "lust" portion of the *Playboy* interview but to leave out the part where he called Johnson and Nixon liars.

Back in Washington, I spent the night at Blair House, where the Carters were staying. The next day I chatted with Rosalynn when she visited the transition office, where Ann was working as Mary Hoyt's assistant. Rosalynn laughed and said, "Pat, I've never seen you in a necktie before." True enough. I'd only worn a tie twice during the campaign: when I was interviewed on national television at the convention, and the morning we visited Warm Springs.

I told Rosalynn I'd just listened to the tapes of her and Carter speaking to the crowd in Plains at dawn the morning after the election. I said how moving I thought both of them had been.

"I couldn't help crying," she said. "Just as we got there the sun came up. The night before, at the rally in Atlanta, I tried to cry. We'd worked so hard and we'd finally won, but I just couldn't. But when I saw all our friends waiting for us and the sun coming up, I couldn't help it."

Carter's collection of speeches, which, at my urging, he called *A Government as Good as Its People*, was published a few months later. The *New York Times Book Review* carried a front-page review of it by Arthur Schlesinger, Jr., the historian and Kennedy loyalist, who churned out several thousand words and concluded that the new president was a conservative, a demagogue, and rather dull.

The transition was an ugly time. In theory, we were seeking the nation's finest talent and planning the bold new policies we would pursue. In reality, we were engaged in a bloody power struggle as old debts were settled and the passions that for months had been directed outward were turned inward as the victors fought over the spoils of war.

Jack Watson made the mistake of challenging Hamilton for power, or seeming to, whereupon Carter sided with Hamilton, and Jack was subjected to the usual anonymous leaks about his loss of influence ("a walking dead man," "emasculated") and had to settle for a secondary White House post. You could certainly make a case that Carter tossed a second term out the window the day he decided to make Hamilton his chief of staff. Compare Ronald Reagan four years later, reaching out to a rival's campaign manager, the brilliant James Baker, for a chief of staff.

Amid this high-level strife, my own situation seemed simple enough. I'd earned the White House speechwriting job and I assumed it was mine if I wanted it. In my mind, the question was whether I wanted the job.

I was sick of Jimmy Carter. I didn't think I was humble enough to be his speechwriter. I wasn't sure anyone was. The campaign had been a wonderful adventure, but the White House would be a bureaucracy, and I knew that the same qualities that had made me a good campaign speechwriter would also make me a lousy bureaucrat.

Jody and I had a couple of inconclusive talks about how my speechwriting operation might fit in the organization chart he was drawing up. I assumed that he and Carter would want me under his direction, but I wasn't sure I could settle for less than one of the top jobs as a special assistant to the president. I had a Washington-wise friend who said, "It doesn't matter what your title is, if you're the president's speechwriter power flows your way." He was right, of course.

The job had its attractions. There was always the hope of doing some good in the world; my fantasies ranged from reuniting the Beatles to helping free a lot of people from jail who didn't belong there. Joe Califano argued that I had to do it so I could write the great Washington novel. The biggest attraction, of course, was that the White House is an ego trip. There are fancy dinners and junkets on Air Force One. They put your name in the papers and plenty of jet-setters and media celebrities want to be your friend. The trouble was, I'd had a taste of that on the campaign and I didn't like it.

I was not some bright-eyed lad from Georgia. I'd lived around Washington for fifteen years and I knew the city well. It attracts some terribly bright people, some of whom do important work, but it is also a cynical, superficial, hypocritical city, a cruel city, made all the more so by the distance between its promise and its reality. I'd been in and out of the political world without ever being comfortable there. Writing speeches was easy; playing the political game was not. It had been an extraordinary experience to spend those months writing for the next president, a man I truly believed might bind up the nation's wounds. To have played that role was a rare privilege, one that in retrospect far outweighs the personal frustrations that are part of any campaign. But the campaign was over and the prospect of being lionized because I was Jimmy Carter's speechwriter held little thrill for me. I had a life of my own I could return to. Still, the White House is not something you casually walk away from, so I went through the motions, with no idea what might happen next.

I was in the process of figuring out that I was a writer, not a politician. I had blundered into the political world but never really belonged there. Writers and politicians don't think the same; they define truth differently. I had always been as much spy as speechwriter. I had penetrated the forbidden kingdom, and I always knew I would send back a report to my own people, if only a message in a bottle.

During the transition I tried to steer some of my friends into the administration. Just how jobs were filled was a mysterious process, but Hamilton was central to it, and I was on good terms with his deputy, Landon Butler. One day I took Landon to lunch with my friend Ruth Prokop, who wound up as general counsel of the Department of Housing and Urban Development. Others I pushed included Bowman Cutter, who became the number-two man at the Office of Management and Budget, Carol Tucker Foreman, who became an assistant secretary of Agriculture, Alan Novak, who was appointed to the Commission on Fine Arts, and Steve Friedman, who went to the Treasury Department and later was an SEC commissioner. These were outstanding people who might well have been selected without my help, but at that point being my friend didn't hurt.

After a decent interval, I called Dave Kennerly in the White House and reminded him of our "winner buys dinner" bet.

"I owe you dinner," I said.

"I wish to hell I owed you dinner," Dave said glumly.

The comic highlight of the transition came when a woman I knew, who was active in the liberal wing of Northern Virginia politics, invited me to lunch and said I should consider running for the Senate in the upcoming election, which was eventually won by the team of John Warner and Elizabeth Taylor. I began to protest, but she said, "Just listen. You're good-looking, you've got a beautiful family, you're articulate, you'd be coming out of the White House—why not?" Soon I was caught up in her fantasy. Later that afternoon, I told Ann what our friend proposed.

My wife began to laugh.

"Wait a minute," I protested. "Susan says . . ."

"Susan doesn't know you as well as I do," Ann said, and that ended my political career.

Jim Fallows wasn't interested in being the number-two White House speechwriter; he planned to talk to Stu about an issues job. Meanwhile, résumés were pouring in. One of President Ford's writers wrote to say that he certainly liked the White House and would like to be considered for the Carter team. I added his letter to my Audacity File.

I hoped to hire Bob Maynard, an editorial writer for the Washington *Post*, whom I'd met through our mutual friend, Keith Stroup of NORML. Bob was an elegant, brilliant, sardonic man of about my age who'd come up the hard way, on Afro-American newspapers, before the big dailies started hiring blacks. He'd won a Neiman fellowship to Harvard, then joined the *Post*, and he headed a program to help young blacks into mainstream journalism. Carter had talked a lot about bringing outstanding blacks into government and I thought it would be a coup if I could hire Bob. We had lunch in mid-December and he expressed guarded interest.

I was eager to tell Carter about Maynard and I had a chance on December 28 when he met with his Cabinet appointees and senior staff during a visit to St. Simons Island in Georgia. I chatted with Joan Mondale on the flight down. We talked about her children and I asked what they read. "Oh, my children don't read," she told me.

Our destination was the Musgrove Plantation, a spectacular estate owned by a tobacco-company heir named Smith Bagley. Once you entered the gates of Musgrove Plantation, you knew the revolution was over.

There was a buffet that night in a huge, lodge-like building. The Cabinet appointees and their wives were ill at ease, but Greg and I discovered there was excellent wine at the bar and we grabbed a few bottles for prompt consumption. A certain macho overtakes you after a campaign like ours. We were swaggering, battle-scarred veterans who'd saved America from Gerald Ford. A grateful nation owed us its finest wines and its virgin daughters. We viewed the Cabinet appointees, with their starched shirts and nervous wives, with the casual contempt that the warrior must always feel for the noncombatant.

Moving about the room, I told Ted Sorensen, who had been nominated to head the CIA, about my friend Sam Adams, a CIA analyst who'd been fired for protesting the agency's doctoring North Vietnamese troop figures. I hoped Sam could get his job back, and Ted promised to look into it, but his own appointment was soon shot down because of his liberal/pacifist background.

I had a discouraging talk with David Berg, a Houston lawyer who was fighting for a generous program to enact Carter's oft-promised pardon for Vietnam-war resisters. He had attended a meeting at which the fine print was discussed, and Charles Kirbo had taken a hard line. Fritz Mondale, whom David had counted on for support, had remained silent. "Mondale," he said bitterly. "Mondale has the *soul* of a vice president."

I spoke to Hamilton about my friend Carol Tucker Foreman, a consumer activist whose appointment as an assistant secretary of Agriculture was under fire from the food industry. "I'd say that speaks well for her," Hamilton drawled. "I hope she takes the job." And he wandered away, enigmatic as always.

Carter arrived and worked the crowd, grinning broadly, pumping the hands of his appointees and kissing their wives with abandon. Eventually he and I talked. It was an ego trip, of course, to stand there nose to nose with the president-elect while the Cabinet types watched enviously. Needless to say, it looked better than it was.

I told Carter, with some enthusiasm, about my hope of hiring Bob Maynard. To my dismay, he scowled.

"Has he ever written any speeches?" he demanded.

I confessed I didn't know.

"I don't want you to hire anyone who's never written a speech for me."

"Governor, *I'd* never written a speech for you," I protested, but he ignored my logic.

"I want you to have anyone you're interested in hiring write me a draft of an inaugural speech," he added.

I thought that was insane, but I let it pass. Soon Carter moved on to brighten the lives of others.

The more I thought about Carter's reaction to Bob Maynard, the more I feared I knew what the trouble was. Bob had been one of the panelists on the second debate. And Bob had this problem: He talked like God. I remembered him asking Carter some tough questions about black unemployment in that booming, repent-your-sins voice of his. But surely Carter wouldn't hold that against him.

Or would he?

I decided to leave. Outside, someone introduced me to Bert Lance.

This man had been the best-kept secret of the campaign. I'd never seen nor heard of him. Carter's inner circle must have viewed him as the half-wit brother who has to be locked in the cellar when company comes.

Lance and I shook hands, gazed into each other's eyes, and it was loathing at first sight. He was the kind of big, bluff, bullshitting, back-slapping, back-stabbing, mush-mouthed professional country boy who makes my skin crawl. Soon he would be Carter's budget director, and all the world would know of Bert Lance's charming ways and creative banking techniques.

The next morning Carter returned to the lodge to meet with his Cabinet. He began by declaring that he intended to keep his commitments to the American people: "My personal honor is at stake!" He said his election had raised hopes around the world, and it was imperative that "we make giant strides toward peace." Carter told his appointees that he wanted to learn from them, that each of them had special talents to contribute, that he invited their criticisms and wanted to work with them as equal partners.

I scribbled: "JC's repeated assertions of equality only underscore their secondary role."

Secretary of State–designate Cy Vance made a little speech about how honored they all were to serve in the Carter Cabinet. Each of the others followed with his or her own little speech. Finally Fritz Mondale rather wistfully asked the Cabinet not to forget about him.

Carter lectured them on efficiency in government. He said he wanted a 30 percent cutback in the White House staff. He said there were 325 color television sets in the White House, and that "the Signal Corps hauls 60 telephones everywhere the President goes, and I think this is disgusting!"

Zbig, who was to be the national-security adviser, suggested there be a program to set out the goals of the Carter administration.

I whispered to Greg, "We could call it Goals for America!"

Greg and I knew, and we thought Zbig did too, that as governor Carter had sponsored a much-publicized Goals for Georgia program. But Carter only nodded and said that was an excellent idea.

On the flight back to Washington, Greg told me about a problem he faced. Before he joined the campaign, he'd owned a bar that failed and left him with a lot of debts, not all of which had been paid. Moreover, he'd collected unemployment insurance at a time when he was starting a restaurant-consulting business, which might have been a technical violation of the law.

Greg said this had come to light during the FBI's routine investigation of him for a White House job. Carter was informed, and now Greg was talking to Hamilton and Kirbo, who would advise Carter. (Carter had declared, "I can't have a Watergate on the eve of my inauguration!") Greg was resigned to not being the presidential appointments secretary, and the question was whether he'd get a lesser job or any job at all. All this was starting to leak to the press, he said.

Greg and Marie were to be married two nights later, on New Year's Eve. They were among several staff couples who were marrying after Carter suggested that matrimony was preferable to living in sin. Now Greg didn't even know if he had a job when he returned from his honeymoon. He was depressed; we both were. We talked about the pettiness of the political world and whether the moments of glory justified all the crap you had to endure.

Why was this very minor matter leaking to the press? Were Ham and/
or Jody using it to shoot down Greg? I remembered Jody calling Greg a
"suckass" two months earlier, when Greg crossed him. Greg mentioned
the name of a nice young Georgian who'd sat out the campaign but now
was likely to get the job that he had earned. Jody and Ham liked nice
young Georgians.

Once, during the campaign, a reporter commented on how quickly I'd
been admitted to Carter's "inner circle." He was wrong. I had access to
Carter, but the inner circle was made up of a very small number of Georgians: Rosalynn, Jody and Ham, Kirbo and Lipshutz, Bert Lance, and
maybe one or two others. They'd run Georgia for four years, they'd run
the campaign, and now they were ready to run the world. What need had
they for "outsiders"?

On New Year's Eve, the night of Greg and Marie's wedding, Ann and I
checked into the Hay-Adams and went for a drink with a friend, a liberal
lawyer. Our friend, it developed, was furious with Carter for raising the
hope that he might make Frank Johnson, a courageous federal judge in
Alabama, his attorney general, and then appointing his friend Griffin Bell.

"Damn him, he blew in our ear," my friend raged. "All the time he was
just blowing in our ear."

We proceeded to the wedding, then to the dinner and dance that followed at the Sulgrave Club. Jody and Nan were there, and I confronted
him about Greg's problem with the FBI report. "What's the matter with
Carter?" I demanded. "This is chickenshit stuff!"

Jody replied that it was a serious matter and he was deeply concerned
about it. Jody possessed the gift of ambiguity, and I couldn't tell if he
meant he was concerned that Greg would lose his job or that Carter would
be embarrassed.

While I had him captive, I said I thought Carter's idea that I have
potential speechwriters draft an inaugural address was crazy.

Jody only smiled. From his perspective, Jimmy Carter did a lot of crazy
things, and he only concerned himself with the very big ones.

The night drifted on. Music was playing, champagne was flowing, and
we all danced our way into 1977.

One year earlier, at our New Year's Eve dinner in Key West, I'd predicted that Carter would be the next president.

Incredibly, I'd been right, and now I was about to enter the White House with him.

Strange, then, that I was so unhappy.

10

HE MET ME AT THE DOOR WITH HIS BIBLE IN HIS HAND

On Sunday morning, January 2, I was playing tennis when I was summoned for a phone call. I'd sent Carter a first draft of the inaugural speech a few days earlier, and I thought he might be calling about it. Instead it was Ann, and she was upset.

"Mary Hoyt called," she said. "She just came back from meeting with Rosalynn in Plains about the East Wing staff. Jimmy says he has a rule against husbands and wives working on his staff, and I can't work for Rosalynn because you're going to be his speechwriter. Rosalynn went and talked to him but he wouldn't budge."

"Good old Jimmy," I sighed.

"What are you going to do?" Ann asked.

"I can't do anything right now, because he's in church," I said. "Let's talk when I get home."

On the drive home, I realized there was nothing to talk about. It would be dishonorable to take my job at Ann's expense. I thought Carter's "policy" was stupid and sexist. If he could see that, perhaps we could work this out; otherwise it was time to leave the circus. Rosalynn had said if Ann couldn't work at the White House because of her husband's policy, she would see that Ann got a good job at one of the agencies. We discussed that option, but Ann was hurt to have the White House suddenly denied her, and I thought she deserved better treatment.

I called Carter that afternoon. Rosalynn answered and we chatted for a moment, but not about the husband-and-wife problem. That, we both knew, would have to be settled by the menfolks.

Carter and I talked about the inaugural. He said he hadn't read my draft yet, but he'd been reading all previous inaugurals and he thought Kennedy's and Wilson's first were best. He said he'd start a draft soon and it was important to keep it short.

I mentioned Bob Maynard again, but Carter said impatiently that Maynard was pompous. He added that if Maynard would write an inaugural draft he'd look at it.

"Ann told me what Mary said about your husband-and-wife policy," I said.

"Yes, that's always been a policy of mine," he said.

"I must say it strikes me as arbitrary and discriminatory. You're saying someone can't have a job she's qualified for because of who she's married to. It's not much different from saying you won't hire a black or a Jew."

"It's what I think best," Carter replied.

"Well, I wish you'd reconsider. It puts me in a difficult position. Ann's very fond of Rosalynn and excited about working for her."

He didn't reply, so I bit the bullet.

"Governor, if one of us has to give up our job, it might be best if Ann stayed and I went back to my own writing."

He hesitated. When he spoke he seemed genuinely surprised. "I don't want you to do that, Pat."

"I don't want to see my wife treated badly."

"I don't mean to treat Ann badly. I hardly know Ann."

"Well, I wish you'd reconsider your policy. It strikes me as arbitrary and discriminatory and ridiculous."

"It's been my experience that when you have married couples working in a small space, it causes intrigue and gossip," he explained.

"Governor, the White House isn't such a small space," I said. "And I think probably married people cause less gossip and intrigue than unmarried people."

We went back and forth like that. It was so damn stupid. Were Ann and I supposed to get a divorce so we could both work for him? That wasn't going to strengthen the American family, was it?

Finally we returned to the inaugural speech. He asked me to call him about it on Tuesday. He said we both should give more thought to the husband-and-wife problem, and we could discuss it again.

I told Ann what I'd done. She hugged me, and at least a few of my sins were forgiven. But after a moment, she looked concerned. "Pat, you can't bluff the president-elect."

I had to laugh. "Sweetheart," I said, "I just did."

Or had I? A poker player never bluffs unless he can afford to lose, and at that point I no longer cared.

I went into my study and made some notes. I even ventured a prediction: "My guess is he'll admire me for standing up for my wife."

That night we went to a party at Jay and Carol Foreman's house. A lot of political people were there, and I found myself being introduced as Jimmy Carter's speechwriter. I wanted to yell, "*Bullshit! I'm not anybody's anything!*" One woman said, "Oh, you wrote *The President's Mistress*, didn't you? I loved it." I almost kissed her.

I called Carter from the transition office on Tuesday, and we talked about the inaugural. When I suggested there were other speeches we should be thinking about, he interrupted me.

"I interpreted your remarks the other day to mean you'd rather Ann work for Rosalynn than you work for me."

"I do think you should reconsider your husband-and-wife policy."

"No, I talked to Jody and Ham and Bob Lipshutz, and we all agreed there ought to be no husband-and-wife teams in the White House."

"Well, I think it's an unwise policy."

"Yes. And discriminatory and ridiculous, I believe you said."

"All those things. I think if you'd search your soul you'd agree."

It was perhaps an impudent remark, but Carter reputedly prayed many times each day, and I couldn't help thinking that if he sought God's advice, God would surely tell him to cut out this sexist crap.

"I can see how strongly you feel," he continued. "So I think it would be best if Ann works for Rosalynn, and I'll get Jim Fallows to do my speechwriting. I spoke with him, and he's interested."

I was starting to catch up.

"If that's what you want," I said.

"I'm not going to change my policy."

"Fine," I said. "I can handle it either way."

"I wish you'd consider coming in from time to time to do a speech or a project on an ad hoc basis. And I'd like you to consider writing a major history of my administration. Something like Arthur Schlesinger's book on Kennedy. You could have full access to me."

I said that was an interesting idea. He asked if I'd come to Plains on Saturday to discuss both the inaugural speech and the book. I said I would, he thanked me, I thanked him, and that was that.

He had sandbagged me, of course. But it wasn't as if I hadn't asked for it.

I told Ann what had happened.

"It's the best thing," she said. "You'd have been miserable. You couldn't have put up with all that nonsense."

It was true. All that fall, I could see us winning the election, but I could never see me in the White House. Let's face it. I *did* have a problem with authority.

I called Jody and told him I wouldn't run to the papers with news of my departure. I wanted to leave as quietly as possible. The stories about Greg had started to break, and Carter didn't need another story about staff problems. I added that it would be hard for Jim Fallows to step in at the last moment, and I'd give him all the help I could.

"That's damn good of you," Jody said. "I thought about asking you, but I wasn't sure how you'd feel."

I laughed. "Jody," I said, "I feel great."

That afternoon, Joe Duffey, one of the few unabashed liberals in the campaign, called to say he'd been offered the job of assistant secretary of state for cultural affairs. "It seems awfully far out of the mainstream," he worried.

"Joe," I said, "in this administration, the farther out of the mainstream the better."

I flew to Plains on Friday, spent a dispiriting night at Faye's Barbecue Villa, and turned up on Carter's doorstep at nine on Saturday morning. He greeted me in a tie and cardigan sweater, explaining that he was having a news conference at ten to announce that he was sending Fritz Mondale around the world.

He led me into the formal sitting room beside the front door. We sat in two wing chairs by the bay window. Carter produced a small tape recorder, turned it on, and put it on the table between us. Its purpose was not explained.

We talked about the inaugural. He said he'd drawn on my draft, plus material from various others, to produce his own draft.

"What I did was write ideas down on three-by-five cards," he explained. "Then I shuffled them around until I had the right order, then had Maxie type them up. She has a copy at the press office. I wish you'd read it and give me your suggestions."

He gave me his pile of backup material and asked me to see if there were any good ideas he'd missed. He pointed to one thick memo. "That one's from Pat Caddell. It must run fifteen pages. He called and dictated it over the phone for two hours. I don't know why anybody would waste money like that."

He also showed me a draft inaugural that a man in Houston had sent to Kirbo, over the transom, and Kirbo had passed on to him. He said it contained some good phrases, and I promised to look at it. We agreed I'd work on the speech all day and return that night.

We talked about the speech collection. I said I thought I'd edited it down to a reasonable length.

"What do you suggest I do?"

"You can either go through the material and see if I've edited it to your satisfaction," I said, "or you can trust me and send it on to the publisher."

"Let's do that," he said. "Will they object if I want to make changes later?"

"They won't object to anything you want to do."

"Good."

"That's about all I've got to discuss," I said. "Except my own situation and the book you proposed."

Carter waited for me to continue. His little tapes were spinning.

"I think this has worked out for the best," I said. "I'm not cut out for staff work. I'm too independent."

"I noticed that, Pat. You're so rigid and demanding. Sometimes I didn't know if you were working for me or I was working for you."

We both made smiles, and he quickly added, "Of course, it's good to have people who are independent."

He talked about the book on his administration, and he stressed that I would have extensive access to him. He used the Kennedy-Schlesinger analogy again. I did not point out that when Schlesinger wrote his book on Kennedy, Kennedy was dead. I told him I might focus on his first year in office and compare the promise of the campaign to the reality of his performance.

He said, "You know, I don't mind you making money from this book. I hope you make a lot of money."

"It could be a big book," I ventured.

"But I wonder if you'd consider donating some percentage of your profits to the Jimmy Carter Foundation."

I expressed concern that such an arrangement might compromise the book, but that did not impress him, so I said I would talk to my agent about it.

Then, because I had nothing to lose, I said, "Governor, did you have any particular percentage in mind?"

"No, no," he said. "You could think about that."

I asked how we would announce my departure. "It's starting to leak, but I didn't want to say anything until I spoke to you."

I thought he might say something at his news conference, toss a few compliments my way, mention the book he wanted me to write, and thus discourage the inevitable stories that I'd been forced out.

Instead he said, "Just tell them that Ann's going to work for Rosalynn and you're going to write a book."

I drove to the Best Western and told Charlie Mohr of the *Times* I was leaving because I wanted to return to my own writing. I'd decided not to mention the husband-and-wife policy unless a reporter brought it up. I thought it made Carter look like an idiot, and I feared that if the stories of my departure embarrassed him it would cost Ann her job.

That afternoon David Broder of the Washington *Post* called and said he'd heard I was leaving because of a "conflict of personalities" with Carter and because some Carter people were embarrassed by *The President's Mistress*. I told Broder that was ridiculous and urged him to call Jody. That was the height of my naïveté, since Jody was almost certainly his source in the first place.

I spent the afternoon on the speech. Carter's draft had some good ideas but was disorganized and themeless. Given the nature of his campaign, I thought Carter's theme should be "the people"—that he'd gone to the people, listened to them, owed everything to them, and so forth. My opening line had been, "Once again the people have spoken."

Carter had cut that and had written a new opening that I read with dismay:

"I have just taken the oath of office on a Bible my mother gave me many years ago—opened to an admonition and a promise from God to King Solomon, still applicable to our people, our leaders, and our great nation.

"'If my people, which are called by my name, shall humble themselves, and pray, and seek my face, and turn from their wicked ways, then will I hear from heaven, and will forgive their sin, and will heal their land.'"

It sounded to me as if Carter was confusing himself with King Solomon or perhaps with God. In my memo to him, I put the case more gently:

"I like the opening reference to the Bible, but I question whether that particular biblical quotation is appropriate. It could be interpreted as your suggesting that the American people humble themselves and turn from their wicked ways and their sins, but you've been arguing all along that the government was bad and the people were good."

I returned to Carter's home at seven. As we settled in the parlor, a phone rang somewhere in the house. After three rings, Carter called out, "Amy! Your phone's ringing!"

The ringing stopped. Carter looked at me.

"Did you hear that?"

I said I did.

"I have very sensitive ears," he said. "Sometimes I think I'm the only one around here who can hear."

As Carter read my memo and my new draft of the speech, his son Jack wandered in. Jack was a big, beefy lawyer who hadn't been very visible on the campaign. He sat down cross-legged on the floor. After a while he said, "You're gettin' kinda shaggy."

I took that as a reference to my hair. "That's what happens," I told him, "when you work hard and don't have time to get haircuts."

Jack chewed on that a while, then vanished from my life forever.

Carter finished my memo.

"You didn't like my biblical quotation," he said.

I said that was true.

"Pat," he began, "are you . . . ?"

He stopped and started over.

"I *assume* you are a Christian."

Rather than confess my godless state, I only smiled.

"Well, we Christians believe in original sin, and therefore . . ."

He delivered a little sermon, the point of which was that his biblical quotation was entirely proper and could not possibly be misunderstood by anyone.

When he finished, I said, "It's up to you. I just think it will sound pious and moralistic to some people."

He said that he had planned to take the oath of office on the Bible his mother gave him but that Mayor Beame of New York had offered him the Bible that George Washington had used. He asked my opinion, and I said he should stick with his mother's Bible. As it turned out, he used them both.

He asked my opinion of the unsolicited inaugural the man in Houston had sent. I said I thought it was awful. Carter frowned. He liked the unknown Texan's soaring rhetoric. Eventually he used a few lines, whereupon the fellow called the White House demanding credit.

Carter said he'd work on the speech that night and asked if I'd return the next morning, before he went to church. I said I would, although I was rapidly losing interest. If Jimmy Carter wanted to deliver a half-assed inaugural address, that was his problem. I wanted to go get drunk.

I walked to the Secret Service trailer at the end of the block to make a copy of his draft. On my way back, I cut across Carter's front yard. Suddenly a man was shining a flashlight in my face.

"I'm staff," I said, pointing to my staff pin.

"You'll get yourself shot if you don't watch out," the agent grumbled.

I laughed helplessly. That would be a fitting end to this fiasco: for me to be gunned down by the Secret Service in Jimmy Carter's front yard.

The next morning I called a friend in Washington to see how the papers had handled my departure. As often happens, the New York *Times* and the Washington *Post* seemed to be reporting two different events.

Charlie Mohr's piece said I was leaving to resume my own writing, used Carter's "I didn't know if you were working for me or I was working for you" quote, which I'd given Charlie, made me out as more of an intimate of Carter's than I'd ever considered myself, and even carried a good picture of me.

David Broder's piece in the *Post* quoted me as saying I wanted to return to my own writing, then quickly rebutted me: "Others close to the situation say there was a 'conflict of personalities' and some sensitivity on the part of Carter insiders to the publicity given Anderson's mildly 'gamy' novel being the work of Carter's speechwriter."

The bit about my novel was absurd—Jody was scraping the bottom of the barrel on that one—but I rather liked the 'conflict of personalities' line. Anyone who didn't have a conflict of personalities with Carter didn't have a personality.

Still, it was typical of the Carter operation that although I'd done everything I could to leave quietly they just had to put the knife to me.

I returned to Carter's house at nine-thirty, as he'd requested. He met me at the door with his Bible in his hand. He explained that he was preparing the lesson for his Sunday-school class. He gave me his latest draft of the inaugural and asked me to read it while he continued work on the Sunday-school lesson.

I read the speech, which was still disorganized and themeless. After a while he returned and asked if I wanted to stay and work on the speech while he was in church.

"Do you have a typewriter?" I asked.

"No."

"I couldn't do much without a typewriter. I've made some notes in the margins. The question is how you want to proceed. It's an important speech. If you like, I'll stay down here and work on it and fly back to Washington with you on Tuesday."

"No. I'd like to work on it by myself for a while."

It was time for him and Rosalynn to go to church. He went for his coat and I waited by the front door. Rosalynn came out and seemed embarrassed to see me. I complimented her bright blue coat. Carter returned, and the three of us walked toward their waiting car.

"I met a friend of yours last night," I said.

"Who was that?" Carter asked.

"I don't remember his name. A husky fellow with a crew cut who said he hunts with you."

Carter's face brightened. He told me the man's name.

"He seemed like a nice fellow," I said.

"Oh, he's a *great* guy!" Carter declared. His voice became high-pitched, the way it did when he was trying to show enthusiasm. "He's Rosalynn's cousin. His granddaddy and her granddaddy were brothers."

"Yes, that's what he said."

We reached the two cars waiting in their driveway: the one they would ride in and another filled with Secret Service men.

"Well, I'll see you," I said.

"You call Maxie if you have any ideas on the speech," Carter said.

"I will," I said, although I doubted I'd be having any more ideas about his inaugural address.

They entered their car. I started across the lawn to my own. A moment later they roared past, on their way to the nearby Plains Baptist Church.

Jimmy Carter was going to Sunday school.

I was going home.

11
A SHADE OF DIFFERENCE

My story properly ends there, as I parted with Carter that Sunday morning in January of 1977. I was off the plane, out of history, a private citizen again, while my comrades from the campaign marched on to run the world.

They did not do an outstanding job of it, and the question that may still be asked, even at this late date, is what went wrong? Why did Jimmy Carter, after coming out of nowhere to capture the presidency, then self-destruct so totally?

Journalists have mostly blamed Carter's defeat on a dismal economy, the hostage crisis in Iran, and the political inevitability of Ronald Reagan. Political scientists have cited his micromanagement, lack of vision and/or the ability to communicate one, and inability or unwillingness to play the Washington political game.

My own view is that Carter's downfall arose from even more basic, more personal reasons that had to do with his unique blending of religion and pride. He was always a flawed hero, one whose strengths and weaknesses were in delicate balance, and most of his weaknesses were visible to those of us around him in 1976, even as we hoped for the best.

Carter, as I have said, was above all else a different candidate, and different most of all because of his oft-proclaimed morality. This was the candidate who first became famous for vowing that he would never tell a lie just to become president—a simple but stunning declaration. The man was either a saint, a fool, or the most insidious liar of all. Whichever, he captured our attention. And, as his neighbors in Plains warned, everyone loved Jimmy for the first hour. He was very lucky, in 1976, to make that first hour stretch out until Election Day.

For all his skill at reaching out to others, Carter remained profoundly different from most of us. The differences were partly religious and partly cultural—sometimes funny and sometime scary—and often hard to put your finger on. But as the differences surfaced, people became more and more uncertain about the many-sided Georgian. Our friends in the media were the first to focus on Carter's oddities, although most of them were too minor to be newsworthy. By midsummer the reporters' nicknames for the candidate were Weirdo and Crater; the latter, transposing two letters in his name, suggested that he was just a bit *off*, a bit *miswired*. They were amused that he relaxed after a hard day by reading a Spanish translation of the Bible. Or that, as noted, he claimed to have first read *War and Peace* at the age of twelve. From the first, Carter's quirks cried out for *Saturday Night Live* satires or, worse, an opponent like Ronald Reagan to make mincemeat of their pomposity.

At times Carter was utterly inscrutable. Was "ethnic purity" simply verbal showing-off, or a subtle appeal to racism? I noted my uncertainty when he made a possibly insulting remark about the Fords' daughter. Did he *know* what he was saying? Another time, at a rally in West Virginia, he told a dumb joke about some tourists in Miami who started yelling "Hialeah!" (the racetrack) instead of "Hallelujah!" in church. Reporters immediately asked me if he could possibly be unaware that a West Virginia audience might take that as "a Jew joke," since at certain levels of southern humor all visitors to Miami are assumed to be Jews.

I pleaded ignorance and fled, but I understood what the reporters meant. The boys at Billy's gas station would have understood what religion those noisy tourists professed. Didn't he *know*? Was he naïve? Was he crazy? Was he Machiavelli or Mr. Peepers?

Still, he sold himself to America, quite brilliantly, as a kind of lay preacher, and we Americans are tolerant of our preachers, even of their dumb jokes. We listen to their sermons, give them our hard-earned money, allow them to marry and bury us, and in return we ask only that they set a good example for us poor sinners.

And how we love it when they fall from grace!

The *Playboy* interview was at the most obvious level funny—the preacher caught with his pants down—and most people enjoyed it at that level. It was a chance for reporters to write about the weirdness that they'd previously only grumbled about. Yet it was more. Carter's views on sex *were* disturbing. What were we to make of a candidate who believed with all his heart and soul that normal sexual daydreams are a mortal sin for which he must seek God's personal forgiveness? It is a relatively harmless theory, but a man who believes it is profoundly different from the vast majority of American men, and he would do well to keep such a notion to himself if he wants to be president.

In time the controversy died down. He hadn't really *done* anything, except look silly, and Americans are tolerant about religious views, up to a point. Still, politically, the *Playboy* interview had revealed a gulf between Carter and millions of people; from that time forward we lived with the danger that it would reappear and widen and swallow him up.

One does not wish to make light of anyone's religion, at least insofar as it inspires him more to good than to ill. Obviously Carter's religion fueled the incredible drive that propelled this essentially nonpolitical introvert to political success, and it was basic to the idealism and decency that made him attractive to millions who didn't otherwise share his fundamentalist beliefs.

Yet the Baptist religion is a mixed bag. Many of us who grew up with Southern Baptists will not forget the sins they imputed to the rest of the world or the glee with which they would remind you that they would someday be sipping iced lemonade in paradise when you and yours were roasting in hell. I never knew anyone to ask Carter his views on that delicate point, and I assume that his is a more generous theology. Still, his deepest intellectual roots are in that exceedingly harsh, judgmental culture, and it was difficult to read the tortured pieties of the *Playboy* interview and not conclude—for all his protestations—that at the very least he believed himself to have an inside track to the lemonade stand.

Religion and pride are an explosive combination. If you start out assuming you're smarter than everyone around you, your problem can only be compounded by a belief that you also have a straight line to God. Carter spoke often of the sin of pride; it tormented him. His problem was that, no matter how he struggled to be humble—and I believe he truly did try—he just couldn't do it. He only managed to seem hypocritical. For millions of Americans his endless, ill-concealed, eye-popping sanctimony became insufferable; it was not so much the economy or the hostage crisis that cost him the 1980 election, I thought, as it was his maddening piety.

Must not Carter's religion sometimes have seemed a curse as well as a blessing? He made two comments to Scheer that hinted at an inner conflict. Pressed about the "sins" of adultery and homosexuality, he declared that you can't legislate morality, but later he added, defensively, plaintively, that they *were* sins and, "I can't change the teachings of Christ. I can't change the teachings of Christ!"

For one terrible moment, you sensed that Scheer had convinced Carter that running for president would be a lot simpler if he *could* bend Christ's teachings to conform with the realities of the 1970s. But he couldn't. In his mind he didn't care what people did in the bedroom but in his soul he was enslaved by a guilt-ridden, sin-saturated theology that told him that half the country was wallowing in the devil's embrace. It must have been an awful burden, all his own imagined sins and the world's too. But he couldn't change the Bible or change himself, and in time he lost us.

What do we want from our presidents? At a minimum we ask that they be regular guys. That they be, or seem to be, like us. Harry Truman was the ultimate regular guy. Ike was the regular guy as war hero. Even Nixon, a villain of Shakespearean dimensions, could babble about the Redskins and do a fair imitation of a recognizable human being.

For all his political success, Carter was never a regular guy; the sum of his parts never quite added up to that. He called to my mind Norman Mailer's 1951 short story "The Language of Men," in which a fussy GI cook (named Carter, by chance) alienates the men in his company, redeems himself by offering to fight a bigger soldier, but remains an outsider, finally realizing that he'll never speak the language of men.

Carter talked his way into the presidency, yet in some profound way he never learned the language of men. He could moralize but he couldn't shoot the bull. He ran brilliantly against the ghosts of Nixon and Watergate, but once they faded we tired of his preaching and stopped rooting for him. The late-night comics circled like vultures. We laughed when Ronald Reagan said, "There you go again." We liked to see him twitted. Reagan's IQ didn't matter. He was the Chaplin, the Picasso, the Gershwin of Regular Guydom. Presidential campaigns resemble nothing so much as high-school elections. By 1980 Carter was the class grind running against the star quarterback; he never had a chance.

It helped, in understanding Carter, to have known his mother. Miss Lillian was a piece of work: tough, outspoken, shameless, irreverent, glorying in the attention that had finally come her way. She was everything her husband had not been. He was content in Plains; she dreamed of escaping it, and did after his death, as a Peace Corps volunteer in India. He accepted segregation; she shocked her neighbors (and loved it) by advocating it. Some of us viewed the campaign as an endless struggle between Carter's Mama side (impulsive, liberal, a show-off, variously petty and admirable, verbal to a fault) and his Daddy side (cautious, conservative, low-keyed, provincial). It was Carter's mother who taught him the big words and gave him the big books and the big dreams. His father taught him whatever he knew about reality, reticence, balancing the books, the language of men. Early in the campaign, his Mama side, the verbal, gimmicky, show-off, high-wire side, had drawn attention to his candidacy, but by the fall, insofar as his handlers had any impact on him, we were trying to stifle that side of him, because, however colorful, it was so damned unpredictable, so potentially disastrous.

He was so isolated. Once, during the transition, he sent me a handwritten note about some minor matter. It was headed "To Pat Anderson," his standard salutation on such notes. That spared him the unwanted intimacy of "Dear Pat" or "dear" anybody. For public purposes, he would proclaim you his "dear friend" if he'd ever been in the same room with you, or maybe the same state, but in private how could he call someone "dear" for whom he felt no affection? That would be hypocritical, a lie, perhaps a sin.

Forget the big smile. That was a disguise. I imagined him living deep in a cave; you could barely see his eyes gleaming in the shadows. He had grown up in Plains, his mother's son, the smartest kid in town, isolated by his intellect, and he remained isolated by his ego, his pride, his ambition, his religion, his sense of mission, by whatever dreams or demons drove him so relentlessly. He related to other people best in his chosen role of leader, up on a pedestal, a little above the rest of us. As long as we accepted that, everything was fine.

The *Playboy* interview first opened up the mysteries of Carter's inner life and its threat to his political goals. I saw a similar problem when he showed me the quotation about God's admonition to King Solomon, that if his people will humble themselves, and pray, and turn from their wicked ways, then he will forgive their sins and heal their land.

Carter meant no more than what we'd already said about a time of torment and a time of healing, but I thought that biblical quotation was an extremely dangerous way to say it. In my mind's eye, it summoned up a scene from a Cecil B. De Mille spectacular, with the earth cracking open, heathen temples collapsing, flames shooting up, the wicked perishing all over the place, even as Charlton Heston wheels up in his chariot to save Deborah Kerr and Jean Simmons. Great stuff, but not the way to start your inaugural address.

So I suggested that the quotation might conflict with his well-known campaign theme that the people were good and it was the government that needed reforming, and Carter's response was to ask if I was a Christian and to lecture me on Original Sin.

Jody and others talked him out of using that passage in the inaugural, but the story didn't stop there. A week after entering office, Carter spoke to a prayer breakfast and used the King Solomon quotation, and went on to explain that his staff had stopped him from putting it in the inaugural and that he was still indignant about it.

We squelched the King Solomon quote, but other events during the transition were far more important and harmful, none more so than the circling of wagons that took place on key personnel decisions.

To a great extent, it was Carter's Mama side, the colorful, diverse, different, I'll-never-tell-you-a-lie, I-see-an-America side that won him the election. But after the election was won, the Daddy side took over with a vengeance. Ham and Jody were crucial to the Daddy side, the traditional, white male, no-nonsense, South Georgia, politics-as-usual side, as were Charles Kirbo and Bert Lance, a small-town banker whose vision of America had to do with writing unlimited overdrafts and riding in a long black Cadillac adorned with his own personal flag.

Perhaps the reason I instinctively disliked Bert Lance, the one time we met, was that I recognized him as my polar opposite. My rhetorical skills had made me an embodiment of Carter's Mama side, and the gimlet-eyed Lance was the very essence of the Daddy side. Perhaps I sensed that he was moving in and I was moving out. They'd needed the likes of me to jolly the voters, but the big boys were taking over now.

As the transition unfolded, Jody and Ham, with Carter's approval, set about demoting and ousting various persons who'd not been humble enough to suit them. The top women in the campaign were shunted aside because Jody and Ham—and, many would say, Carter—were not comfortable with women who presumed to be political equals. Meanwhile, amiable, unqualified Georgians were named to key posts in the White House and elsewhere.

The specifics no longer matter. It is enough to say that the process was as stupid as it was brutal. Even before his Inauguration, Carter had begun to toss aside a second term, because he and his closest advisers didn't like or trust "outsiders." Why? Was the problem Carter's old nemesis, the sin of pride? Having won the election, did he and his inner circle think themselves invincible?

A question remains, of course. If Carter had surrounded himself by the wisest people in America, would it have mattered, or would he have followed his own stars to the same sad end? Most people who knew Carter would say it wouldn't have mattered, that Jimmy was Jimmy was Jimmy and he wasn't going to change.

If proof of that was needed, it came in the summer of 1979 when Carter rejected a nuts-and-bolts speech on the energy crisis, and instead embraced Pat Caddell's mumbo-jumbo about a national crisis of the spirit.

In his memoirs, with unintended humor, Carter relates that "no staff member was enthusiastic about my plans" and that his vice president was "distraught." Carter calmed poor distraught Fritz Mondale and pressed on. Rather than confront the economy, he preached a sermon that blamed the people for losing faith, for lacking confidence, and said that answers to this spiritual crisis must come not from the White House but from individual Americans.

Three years earlier, working on his acceptance speech, he'd reminded me that "I am one of the American people." Now he was up on the mountaintop and the people were failing him with their lack of faith. This was the infamous "malaise" speech, although he didn't use that word, and after it no one ever took his speeches seriously again.

There is a straight line running from the *Playboy* interview to the King Solomon quote to the "malaise" speech. Each time, Carter was too far in the clouds to understand the impact his words would have, although it was painfully visible to earthbound Sancho Panzas like Jody and Mondale and me.

Carter was having the crisis, not America, but he didn't see that. It wasn't that no one warned him, but he was too proud, too pigheaded to listen. The preacher had overwhelmed the politician. That speech became the defining moment of his presidency. He prayed, he went up to Camp David and consulted with elder statesmen and common folk, and in the end he utterly misread the public mood. He preached at us and we were sick of it. After the speech, as one disaster followed another (firing five Cabinet members, cocaine charges against Hamilton, firing Andy Young, the Iran hostage crisis, the failed rescue mission, the disastrous polls, the Kennedy challenge, the rise of Reagan) he became a pathetic figure.

Rarely in political history has so much pride come before so terrible a fall. If there is such a thing as hell on earth, and there is, Carter surely knew it during the last year of his presidency. He could pray, he could blame the media or blame his Cabinet, but in some corner of his heart he surely knew how abysmally he had failed.

Jody and Carter wrote books, when they were at leisure again, bitterly blaming the media for Carter's downfall. But reporters were tough on him because they were sick of his pettiness and pomposity, just as the public was—if the public hadn't been sick of it, the media wouldn't have piled on. In his last year, Carter was ridiculed when he said he'd discussed nuclear war with Amy, and again over the inane "killer rabbit" episode. Neither should have been a story at all. Reagan could have laughed off either one, as he laughed off far bigger blunders, but Carter could not. He wasn't capable of laughing at himself. That was what made twitting him so delicious. You can certainly make a case that the media was unfair to Carter. So what? It doesn't matter. Presidential politics is brutal, and insofar as it has rules, they have nothing to do with "fairness" and everything to do with the exercise of power and the understanding of human nature. Figure out *those* rules and you get a second term.

With Carter, you keep coming back to his pride. He kept coming back to it. He tried to rid himself of it after losing his first race for governor. He unwisely lectured Scheer about it, telling him that sometimes he prayed twenty-five times a day. I imagined that many of those prayers were for humility, not always granted. At the prayer breakfast soon after he was inaugurated, Robert Shogan reported, "He talked with characteristic intensity about sin and humility," and he noted that Carter had said once again that Christ's most constantly repeated admonition was against pride.

Shogan, who wrote a book about Carter's first hundred days, commented, "If Jimmy Carter can't conquer his pride, at least with God's help he can keep it under control." But could he? Did he? Carter blamed pride for helping him lose his first race for governor, but did he ever blame it for losing the election of 1980? Or was it all the media's fault? One can only wonder at his inner torment. Has he ever had second thoughts? The trouble is, you don't get a second chance at the White House.

His second chance has come as an ex-president. Our ex-presidents tend to get what they want. Nixon wanted to be rehabilitated. Ford wanted to play golf and make money. Bush wanted to be a Texan. Carter, a more complex man, wants . . . what? To be respected? To be loved? To have us say we were wrong? A Nobel peace prize? Whatever his goals, he has performed with dignity and is more admired now than ever before in his strange career. At the very least, as the Reagan magic and the Republican mudslinging fade from memory, Americans are starting to admit that Carter was a better president than we gave him credit for.

Perhaps, as the people in Plains predicted, after all these years we are finally starting to understand him. Perhaps he is starting to understand himself. Who can consider the man's long saga, the intensity of his beliefs, the inner turmoil we can only guess at, the dimensions of his rise and fall—and consider, too, his own pride, his own failings, his own humanity—and not wish Jimmy Carter well?

APPENDIX:
MARTIN LUTHER KING
HOSPITAL SPEECH

Jimmy Carter delivered this speech on June 1, 1976, at the dedication of a new wing of the Martin Luther King Hospital in Los Angeles.

We are here today to honor a man with a dream.

We are here to honor a man who lived and died for the cause of human brotherhood.

Martin Luther King, Jr., was the conscience of his generation.

He was a doctor to a sick society.

He was a prophet of a new and better America.

He was a Southerner, a black man, who in his too short life stood with presidents and kings and was honored around the world, but who never forgot the poor people, the oppressed people, who were his brothers and sisters and from whom he drew his strength.

He was the man, more than any other of his generation, who gazed upon the great wall of segregation and saw that it could be destroyed by the power of love.

I sometimes think that a Southerner of my generation can most fully understand the meaning and the impact of Martin Luther King's life.

He and I grew up in the same South, he the son of a clergyman, I the son of a farmer. We both knew, from opposite sides, the invisible wall of racial segregation.

The official rule then was "separate but equal," but in truth we were neither—not separate, not equal.

When I was a boy, almost all my playmates were black. We worked in the fields together, and hunted and fished and swam together, but when it was time for church or for school we went our separate ways, without really understanding why.

Our lives were dominated by unspoken, unwritten, but powerful rules, rules that were almost never challenged.

A few people challenged them, not in politics but in the way they lived their lives. My mother was one of those people. She was a nurse. She would work twelve hours a day and then come home and care for her family and minister to the people of our little community, both black and white.

My mother knew no color line. Her black friends were just as welcome in her home as her white friends, a fact that shocked some people, sometimes even my father, who was more conventional in his views on race.

I left Georgia in 1943 and went off to the Navy, and by the time I returned home ten years later the South and the nation had begun to change.

The change was slow and painful. After the Supreme Court outlawed school segregation, the wrong kind of politicians stirred up angry resistance, and little towns like mine were torn apart by fear and resentment.

Yet the change was coming. Across the South, courageous young black students demanded service at segregated lunch counters. And in the end they prevailed.

In Montgomery, a woman named Rosa Parks refused to move to the back of the bus, a young clergyman named Martin Luther King joined the protest, and a movement had found its leader.

In 1961, we had a new President, John Kennedy, who responded to the demands of the civil rights movement, and who used the power of his office to enforce court orders at the University of Alabama and the University of Mississippi, and who by the last year of his life was giving moral leadership in the struggle for equal rights.

In August of 1963, Martin Luther King stood on the steps of the Lincoln Memorial in Washington and told a quarter of a million people of his dream for America.

"I have a dream," he said. "I have a dream that one day on the red hills of Georgia, sons of former slaves and sons of former slaveowners will be able to sit down together at the table of brotherhood.

"I have a dream," he said, "that my four little children will one day live in a nation where they will not be judged by the color of their skin but by the content of their character. I have a dream."

And so the dream was born. The challenge was made. The rest was up to America.

Three months after Dr. King's speech, President Kennedy was dead, and we had a new President, a Texan, a man whom many black people distrusted. But soon Lyndon Johnson stood before the Congress of the United States and promised, "We shall overcome!"

Lyndon Johnson carried forward the dream of equality. He used his political genius to pass the Voting Rights bill, a bill that was the best thing that happened to the South in my lifetime. The Voting Rights Act did not just guarantee the vote for black people. It liberated the South, both black and white. It made it possible for the South to come out of the past and into the mainstream of American politics.

It made it possible for a Southerner to stand before you this evening as a serious candidate for President of the United States.

But war came, and destroyed Lyndon Johnson's Great Society. Martin Luther King spoke out against that war. There were those who told him to keep silent, who told him he would undercut his prestige if he opposed the war, but he followed his conscience and spoke his mind.

Then, in the spring of 1968, he went to Memphis to help the garbage workers get a decent wage, to help the men who did the dirtiest job for the lowest pay, and while he was there he was shot and killed.

But his dream lives on.

Perhaps some of you remember the night of Dr. King's death. Robert Kennedy was in Indianapolis, running for President, speaking before a black audience. At that point, on that awful night, Robert Kennedy was perhaps the only white politician in America who could have spoken to black people and been listened to.

Let me tell you what he said.

He said, "What we need in the United States is not division, what we need in the United States is not hatred, what we need in the United States is not violence and lawlessness, but love and wisdom and compassion toward one another, and a feeling of justice toward those who still suffer within our country, whether they be white or whether they be black."

Those words are still true today.

We lost Martin Luther King.

We lost Robert Kennedy.

We lost the election that year to men who governed without love or laughter, to men who promised law and order and gave us crime and oppression.

But the dream lived on.

It could be slowed, but never stopped.

In Atlanta, a young man named Andrew Young, who had been Martin Luther King's strong right hand, was elected to the Congress of the United States.

All over America, black men and women were carrying the dream forward into politics.

In Georgia, when I was Governor, we appointed black people to jobs and judgeships they had never held before, and one day we hung a portrait of Martin Luther King, Jr., in our State Capitol.

There were protests, but they didn't matter. Inside our State Capitol, Coretta King and Daddy King and Andy Young and I and hundreds of others joined hands and sang "We Shall Overcome."

And we shall.

I stand before you a candidate for President, a man whose life has been lifted, as yours have been, by the dream of Martin Luther King.

When I started to run for President, there were those who said I would fail, because I am from the South.

But I thought they were wrong. I thought the South was changing and America was changing. I thought the dream was taking hold.

And I ran for President throughout our nation.

We have won in the South, and we have won in the North, and now we come to the West and we ask your help.

For all our progress, we still live in a land held back by oppression and injustice.

The few who are rich and powerful still make the decisions, and the many who are poor and weak must suffer the consequences. If those in power make mistakes, it is not they or their families who lose their jobs or go on welfare or lack medical care or go to jail.

We still have poverty in the midst of plenty.

We still have far to go. We must give our government back to our people. The road will not be easy.

But we still have the dream, Martin Luther King's dream and your dream and my dream. The America we long for is still out there, somewhere ahead of us, waiting for us to find her.

I see an America poised not only at the brink of a new century but at the dawn of a new era of honest, compassionate, responsive government.

I see an American government that has turned away from scandals and corruption and official cynicism and finally become as decent as our people.

I see an America with a tax system that does not steal from the poor and give to the rich.

I see an America with a job for every man and woman who can work, and a decent standard of living for those who cannot.

I see an America in which my child and your child and every child receives an education second to none in the world.

I see an American government that does not spy on its citizens or harass its citizens, but respects your dignity and your privacy and your right to be let alone.

I see an American foreign policy that is firm and consistent and generous, and that once again is a beacon for the hopes of the world.

I see an American President who does not govern by vetoes and negativism, but with vigor and vision and affirmative leadership, a President who is not isolated from our people but feels their pain and shares their dreams and takes his strength from them.

I see an America in which Martin Luther King's dream is our national dream.

I see an America on the move again, united, its wounds healed, its head high, a diverse and vital nation, moving into its third century with confidence and competence and compassion, an America that lives up to the majesty of its Constitution and the simple decency of its people.

This is the America that I see and that I am committed to as I run for President.

I ask your help.

You will always have mine.

INDEX